Letters For Olson

gathered and edited by
Benjamin Hollander

Spuyten Duyvil
New York City

Acknowledgements

Thanks to Henry Ferrini, for permission to use still images from his film, *Polis is This: Charles Olson and the Persistence of Place.* Should there be any typos or misprints or spacing errors in this book, they are solely the responsibility of the editor, Benjamin Hollander, who extends his apologies to the contributors.

ISBN 978-1-941550-86-1

Library of Congress Cataloging-in-Publication Data

Names: Olson, Charles, 1910-1970, addressee. | Hollander, Benjamin, editor.
Title: Letters for Olson / edited by Benjamin Hollander.
Description: New York City : Spuyten Duyvil, [2016]
Identifiers: LCCN 2015044650 | ISBN 9781941550861
Subjects: LCSH: Olson, Charles, 1910-1970—Correspondence.
Classification: LCC PS3529.L655 Z48 2016 | DDC 811/.54—dc23
LC record available at http://lccn.loc.gov/2015044650

This book is for Kenneth Warren

CONTENTS

Benjamin Hollander

INTRODUCTION

I commissioned these letters, hoping for a depth of response which would echo correspondence with Charles Olson, coming in any form, as if correspondence were, in Kenneth Warren's words, "the seal of the planets upon manifested things, as Paracelsus held. God to planet, like to like, person to person, letter to number, word to idea, and so forth." That is the spirit out of which these letters are offered.

Olson never forgot what the United States post office taught him to do: to understand an urban landscape in terms of not only streets but patterns of street addresses. He knew Gloucester through things like the feel of the streets through his boot soles, and most letter carriers notice all sorts of things: the condition of sprouting plants in a garden, the sleeping dog, the newspaper left over from yesterday on the front porch; the local environment is the prism through which anyone's understanding of the cosmos is filtered. What I think Olson did that was spectacularly successful was twist the prism in his hands all the time, and look through it toward an outer world from a vantage point in the local: the ward, the precinct, the corner of the street, his front steps, and, perhaps, above all, the window in his home that looked out over what many people would say was very ordinary and uninteresting but for him was the threshold to the world.

(John Stilgoe, from Polis is This)

He did not divide up subjects according to what he thought was important and what was not important. He went out and absorbed everything; therefore, I think whatever we see in his poetry originated in a kind of openness to everything and a willingness to be open to everything, that nowadays is increasingly rare in part, I think, because of extremely programmed education.….

(John Stilgoe, from Polis is This)

l

LETTERS FOR OLSON

Etel Adnan

Paris, December 11, 2014

Dear Benjamin,

I am so happy you gave me a chance to speak of Olson, as it made me reread, this time carefully, the Maximus Poems.

Some many months ago that interest was awaken by Ammiel's book, around and about Olson: "A little history." A big history in fact. It came as an illumination. A book of passion carefully advancing like a tide. Page after Page Olson expresses himself anew, while Ammiel does same. I mean we also come closer to him. Of course to find out that Ammiel had an intimate knowlege of his neighbor is intriging! A lucky little boy! I mean it.

9

Rereading the Maximus²
Poems, I read them differently.
I saw Melville all over the book:
the ocean, the waters, fishermen
and their tools, the pleasure to
use this parallel language-work
that any trade uses, and creates.
the proximity of harbors and
sails... so clearly stated.
Here's an Atlantic man for
you, the poet in him knows
that such a fact will be
like a siren song.
        I am amused by the
combination: Maximus of
Gloucester — Shakespear
and the British House
as a constant background
ironically set against
an apology of the working
class. A coincidence, of course,
a humorous one, but still,
much more.

Ammiel's book is a
plea through Olson, the
incorrigible desire to ask
poets to become poets, be
what they used to be
in mythical times: the tribe,
conciousness of the tribe, way,
its memory, in one way,
and the tracing of its
future, in another.
    Olson's very very long
poem and Ammiel's witnessing
study/biography/ so many
book stirred so many
questions, related even if
they appear unrelated:
    —was the Civil war
really about slavery? I
don't think so, and now more
than ever. It was the
classical response of
governments against
the partition of a nation,

11

4

something that would
bring diminution of power
A corollary: would it have
been better if the south
had won, each half of
America evolving
differently, and ultimately,
the atom bomb not
happening? Obviously,
it would have been
a different adventure.
(and, maybe, couldn't
have been worst).
And another question
out of the "little history"
so related to the bigger
one, and with its closeness
to Amiri Baraka:
has, for example, Angela
Davis been invited to
participate in this project,

To give her views, her reactions, her likes and dislikes, concerning Olson, and beyond?

years ago I loved Olson because I considered his Maximus Poems as a sort of "Total" biography of the archetypal dream of any poet // any person. That remains true.

Now, I love the poems, but I love the poet equally: I don't sound (reasonable) I know. I am confirmed in my deep feeling that poets ought to change the world, and they do, regardless if it is noticeable or not.

Ammiel has been discreet. He thought first, things first. But as I wish he also told who used to win at Badminton?

6

dear Benjamin, I can go
on and on. It's so gray
outside, and worst than
that, the streets present
so much junk that the
feast days are rather un-
escapable nightmares.
Olso, had he been alive,
would have been even
more desperate. But we
are not totally desperate,
really not. The minute
details of life, like those
he tells about in his poems,
remain worthwhile. Anyway
they are all we have. But
we have them.
    There are many pages
left for me to read in the
"Maximus". Then I will read
his other books. Thank you
for opening up these possibilities.

XX: the Babylon he was not allowed to visit is simply
gone.

We are, like you know, and as
Jalal Toufic says, in
a period of "a disaster
surpassing disasters" all over
in the U.S. also more than it
wants to know. Olson
would have been appaled,
would have been hitting
his head on the wall.
Now it's many Ahabs against
millions of Moby Dicks...
let me know what
goes on. little lights in a
big night shine
wonderfully. There may be even if
only a few. much much love
to you, Etel

Ricardo Cázares

A Letter for Olson
(From an Unlicensed Spectrometry Lab)

Huixquilucan, Nov. 25, 2014

Dear Olson,
   More yet to tell you   yet, by late two thousand
and 14 we're   no-where? near to finding out a way to
make the damn machine work out,   fr   you,   as
you, intended — still no way to fully measure yr own
μέτρον-*res extensa*, guess?, (at best) *videcilet* yr own
enormous body in one's language. Not

                    a pattern yet in
                         which
                                   to speak or
                         dress/ad-dress
                                        to re-
                              arrange your
                              "mortal soul" (that bit be-
                                   speaks of
                         future laziness, at best

          a sloth of
          rhetoric
          At best, *for* best,   "still looking for a language".......

We go back
to it, to
look for it in
SPACE
            (the way in which
      our body-breath made
      syllable   moves
through IT

(It was Butterick who wrote of you, still looking for the measure of your body in language while you waited for the cancer to kill you.) Spectroscopy. That was the thing. From Latin: *spectrum* "appearance, image, apparition", a "specter" or   a   <u>range</u>; arranged as

"a   continuous-infinite-one-dimensional-set, possibly bounded by extremes" and

σκοπέω "to see".

Then onto it as "measurement of quantity *as* function of wavelength or frequency." As "response to an alternating field or varying frequency ('v')", with ENERGY as variable. I've looked into it, done my own saturation job, re: wavelengths/ application of the same to record the *anima* thru body-mass and breath, and come up empty.

(So the business with the spectroscope's a bust.) Not much help to you at this, or any, stage. But still, there *is* a comfort in one's breath pro-tracting breath. A

blessing, say, or better yet, the "simple" recognition of
the self while words go probing the dark cracks which
men of medicine go over (and secretly detest.)

It's there in *Maximus*
      in every syllable
of song

          (the way in which
the verse, as instrument
probes light over the spectrum
of the real
      the actual reading through
of time in time
projects perception
    ("one perception to
the next")

the wavelength of your breath moving across
from nineteenfifty/fifty-
something until
now
is the chain of resurrection

"the spectral line", they call it

(while visiting your house
    at 28 Fort Square
    at the very edge of
breath moving versus

              breath
         while light cut through
the little waves

(and on down to church
to read a Spanish version of *I,
Maximus of Gloucester, to You*, to read
aloud, for

"one loves only form,
and form only comes
into existence when
the thing is born"

Something like this:

*uno sólo ama la forma,
y la forma sólo llega
a existir cuando
la cosa nace*

              *nace de ti mismo, nace
         del heno y los tallos de algodón,
    de los residuos de la calle, los muelles, la hierba
         que llevas, pájaro mío*

                    *de un hueso de pescado
               de una pajita, o lo hará
         de un color, de una campana
                    de ti mismo, roto*

I distinctly recall the diffraction of light on a single little wave, late at night at Stage Fort Beach. After the marathon reading for the Centennial celebrations was over, the remaining group of younger poets, led by David Rich, went out walking, spotting old olsonian landmarks. I had spent much of the day there with my wife and friends Juan Carlos Cano and Antonio Ochoa, trying to dig up something out of the ground in Dogtown, asking directions to our Lady of Good Voyage, taking some photos outside of your house...................... All this: "romantic/ stuff I promised never to leave life riding on". So it's best to stop that here.

Just this: that a man such as yourself *is* the shape and size of his own content, that THE WORK still exceeds and spills over from your breath. A flow of energy, alive, through/against the pattern of chaos in language/the world/the line which grips the self to hold in place and then   lets go,
of it,   for it to cut
thru field.   THE WORK, dear Olson, still of use, in
any given instance.

You see, I'm still trying to figure out what kind of letter I should write,   to you, 44 years dead, and whom I never met, but know, or think I do, but don't. In any case — too late— and done. Is done. Is said. And sure (am sure) that you won't mind the wobbly verse (too weak the distance measured by it), since it is, you said, that verse is the "time MAKER". Every syllable hemmed, hammed, hammered here, for you. After all, "we measure our masters by "em."

In future company,

Ricardo Cázares

PS:

I'm saving a copy of this letter for my son (2 months old), should he ever wonder why his crazy old man decided to call him Maximus while in an incubator, looking for *the breath*.

Murat Nemet-Nejat

Dear Charles, Letters from a Turk: *Mayan Letters*, Herman Melville and *Eda*

Dear Charles,

I first came across your *Mayan Letters* in 1974 in London as I was browsing a book store, now defunct and whose name I have forgotten, dedicated to poetry and arcane essays and novels—that strange and sweet book where only your side of correspondence with Creeley appears. Subliminally, a clapping with one hand, in which you are searching, reminiscent of a demented alchemist, for a new kind of poetry in the far distant, neglected ruins of a poor, sun-scorched area in Mexico.

Glyph! What a strange, mysterious word to me it was at the time. I had not seen a glyph before. It reminded me of the wind.

Day has let itself be taken by the wind,
it's walking around befuddled.

*

Dear Charles,

I was attending Eric Mottram's London Polytechnic lectures at the time, myself twice removed from my own home, Istanbul and my adopted city New York, and in the middle of writing my first long poem *The Bridge*. Eric had mentioned you, but not *Mayan Letters*. Finding that book was pure happenstance, maybe with inducement from D. H. Lawrence whose poetry and novels I had been reading.

More than any specific ideas about poetry or history you were proposing, what hooked me, what I never forgot in *Mayan Letters* was its strange intimacy, the awkward twists of your prose that made me experience sitting next to you watching you write these letters— *watching* you not necessarily listening to you. Part of me said one should not write this way. It is bad writing. Another part loved you doing it, because I wanted to write the same way (though I did not know it at the time). Your prose thrilled me. Here is a taste of it:

> ... These Maya shure went for vistas... But it's hieroglyphs, which are the real pay-off, the inside stuff, for me. And that's not in situ, that is, you can't see them—why Sánchez is so very much the value, for me, here (he came to dinner Monday night, and by god if he doesn't come in with the whole set of little books published in Campeche with his drawings of same, damnest sweetest

present, and, too much,

as you'd say, too much...

What wilds me, is, that here, in these things, is the intimate art (as against the mass & space of the buildings (god-stuff), and the corn-god, woman temple, sacrifice-stone (the social purpose))

        Or Jaina! Jesus, what work,

there: the only trouble is, they know, and it's guarded, & and for me to dig, no go: have to be an official, have to be what I was talking about, above: just one thing, in Museo, Campeche, two clay things, abt a hand's span all, of the calix of a flower with a human being rising, right where the pistil would be! Incredible delicacy, & sureness: as in the glyphs, only, the glyphs already one stage formal, one stage set: the same glyphs, with variations, fr north to south...[1]

"What wilds you!" Yes, what wilds me in this passage Charles is that it does not represent a crystallized record of ideas or opinions, but the magma of your thoughts as they're occurring, their outflow, pell-mell, almost chaotic as if in a crowded bus. A prose of process. As if in a fluid film strip, one has a picture of

---

1   *Mayan Letters*, Edited and with a Preface by Robert Creeley, Cape Editions: London, 1968, © 1953 by Charles Olson, p. 50/1.

thought hunting for itself, discovering, waiting to see where it will land. A prose of thoughtspirit in motion. A thrilling sight to see.

Yours is a prose of passing moment just before a thought has frozen into fixed shape, an evanescent (free!) moment of the mind, exactly the quality you see in the "clay things" you admire so much, even surpassing your beloved glyphs: "Incredible delicacy, & sureness: as in the glyphs, only, the glyphs already one stage formal, one stage set ."

A vision of *un-formal* prose, one foot subjective, still in the mind; another, entering the world, still retaining the light of the other.

*

Dear Charles,

I am seduced by a contradiction in your work. In the hierarchy of American poetry you are seen—see yourself— as the poet of geography, of space, the wide physical landscape of America. But you project this poetry from the subjectivity of your lungs.

These lungs echo in my mind Moby Dick's lungs as it's swimming the Pacific Ocean—in other words, Moby Dick's breathing *writing* Ahab's globular brain. Moby Dick's motions in the ocean merely a mirror of Ahab's maniacal dreams.

Only indirectly reflecting, together, the mania of American. That's why that odd beast *Moby Dick* is a fusion of encyclopedia and visionary sea tale. Facts act as dreams, dreams become fact. The satyr of a holy black magic.

This is your glorious, dirty secret, Charles. While projecting the image of the opposite—America's wide open space—in your writing prose you're the poet of the "passing moment," of a radical subjectivity. Your faith is that this subjectivity leads to the radically objective, as you suggest in *Call Me Ishmael* that Melville's inner demons end up being America's demons. You quote Melville himself: "I have written a wicked book and feel as spotless as the lamb."[2]

This faith in the objectivity of the passing moment (and of the mind—in your vocabulary the breath—tracing it) and that coupled together they reveal a profound, elusive truth is what thrilled me when I first read *Mayan Letters* in the 1970's. I was an outsider Persian Jew born in Turkey, half in spiritual exile in the West, trying to write, fearing foolishly an American poem. This book about a history and artifacts I knew very little about spoke directly to me. Subliminally it implied that an American work can be written about another place, that national boundaries in an American poem are illusionary—a spiritual borderlessness is the essence of its democracy. *Moby Dick*, which initially I read through the prism of *Call Me Ishmael*, relayed a similar message.

Within the framework of this high, reaffirming the

2   Charles Olson. *Call Me Ishmael*, Grove Press Inc.: New York, 1947, © by Charles Olson, p. 54.

legitimacy of my subjectivity and otherness, that I read the "mighty mildness of repose in swiftness :) "[3] of your language of mental process in *Mayan Letters.* Dear Charles, the experience was liberating, and prophetic. I could see myself writing in this language, being part of this literature. Though I didn't quite know it at the time, it (and reading *Call Me Ishmael*) dimly pointed to a spiritual language consisting of *movements* of thought, thought as linguistic tissue, the poetics called *Eda* that I will develop in the ensuing twenty-five years. Finally, the book implied, though again I wasn't aware of it then, that, freed of psychic boundaries, a poem, a poetics may belong to two cultures, languages simultaneously.

*

An Interjection:

Reference: *Eda: An Anthology of Contemporary Turkish Poetry* (2003)

Ostensibly, *Eda Anthology* delineates a poetics for modern Turkish poetry, the way *Mayan Letters* is about Mayan artifacts. Simultaneously, both are American works, exploring—and discovering— new possibilities for a new spiritual language—of the mind and of the world, subjective and objective—for American poetry. The poetic of *Eda* rests on a trinity

---

3   As Olson points in *Call Me Ishmael*, these are the words Melville uses as Moby Dick appears for the first in his book

of concepts: syntactic (agglutination), thematic (the city of Istanbul as a mistress) and metaphysical (an Asiatic godless Sufism). Here is a passage from the introduction discussing the first, revealing *Mayan Letters* to belong already to *Eda* poetics:

> Turkish is an agglutinative language, that is to say, declensions occur inside the words as suffixes. Words need not be attached to either end of prepositions to spell out relationships, as in English. This quality gives Turkish total syntactical flexibility. Words in a sentence can be arranged in any permutable order, each sounding natural.
>
> The underlying syntactical principle is not logic, but emphasis: a movement of the speaker's or writer's affections. Thinking, speaking in Turkish is a peculiarly visceral activity, a record of thought emerging....
>
> *Eda* is the play of ideas through the body of Turkish. Not only is it the poetics of Turkish poetry in 20th century, it is the extension of the language itself, the flowering of its inherent potentials as a language.[4]

*

---

4   *Eda: An Anthology of Contemporary Turkish Poetry*, edited by Murat Nemet-Nejat, Talisman House, Publishers: Jersey City, New Jersey, 2003, pp. 5/6

Dear Charles,

In *Call Me Ishmael* you quote the pivotal phrase in *Moby Dick* when Pip sees "God's foot on the treadle of the loom" while drowning and reemerges insane opening Ahab's heart, Lear-like, to the sufferings of humanity. Did you know spinning in emulation of a loom, in an ecstasy of tears & desire, is a primary Sufi act to reach God? In the divine processes of *Arcs of Descent and Ascent*[5], falling and rising are one?

Spin o sa

> The rose is a movable mecca spinning
> the marten also
> is spinning,
> but the marten is agile a worker
> on the skyscraper
> of the soul cleaning
> its windows.
> loving vertigo, the marten
> is spinning
> agile and lonely
> wiping
> away. the rose is spinning,
> at the *pit /*
> *c h*
> of the vertigo.[6]

5   See *Eda: An Anthology*, pp. 7/8.
6   Seyhan Erözçelik, *Rosestrikes and Coffee Grinds*, translated

Moby Dick is the key American Sufi work.

In *Eda*, the depths of the Pacific and canyons of Manhattan unify. Water becomes air, drowning and vertigo being expressions of a thirst for an elusive white, an indefinable other.

    ...

    the *great white* crosses and joins the captain's
                  log.
         noticing its own sound,
           the sea gull panics,
           tilts one wing in,
           the weak worm
of *ionized penitence*
in its beak,

              makes *it*
          ice cream, the finicky
        gull   hold the sugar
             cone.
             boy!
"condom an *insult*?"

            ocean
      sunset. (küçük İskender, *souljam*[7])

---

by Murat Nemet-Nejat, Talisman House, Publishers: Greenfield, Massachusetts, 2010, p. 69.
7   Eda: An Anthology, p. 293.

*

Dear Charles,

He [Melville] was like a migrant backtrailing to Asia... some Inca trying to find a lost home." (*Call Me*, p. 14)

... Through these forms that certain sultanisms of Ahab's brain became incarnated in an irresistible dictatorship... (*Call Me*, 65)[8]

The fog lifted from about the skirts of the city [Constantinople]... It was a coy disclosure, a kind of coquetting,... like her Sultanas she was thus seen veiled in her 'ashmak.' (*Call Me*, 94)[9]

Your stunning work of youth on Melville *Call Me Ishmael* draws multiple arcs: from the 19th century recorded documents on whaling ships (objective facts)

---

8   Olson is quoting from "The Specksynder" chapter in Moby Dick.
9   Olson is quoting from the journal Melville kept during his pilgrimage to the Holy Lands after the writing of Moby Dick. He is quoting from obscure, at the time unpublished documents. The fact shows the great importance he attached to them. The journal was first published by Northwestern University Press in 1989 under the title Journals as Volume Fifteen as part of The Northwestern-Newberry Edition of the Writings of Herman Melville.

Passage from the at the time unpublished Journals Melville kept during his pilgrimage to Jerusalem after the writing of Moby Dick, quoted in Call Me Ishmael, p. 94

to *Moby Dick*, from Shakespeare (the plays' texts) to Melville's thoughts on them (his marginal notes), from Melville's migrant being backtrailing to Asia to your own ideas to reclaim a lost home (*The Mayan Letters*).

But, to me, the most stunning arc in *Call Me Ishmael*, the one that speaks directly to me, is the book's submerged, "irresistible" drive to Asia, like a Moby Dick traveling the oceans, from "the sultanism of Ahab's brain" to its sultana: the city of Constantinople (Istanbul)— a shadow Pillars of Hercules in the East, both being the gateways to a new, dangerous unknown and also a home.

Moby Dick to me is an image of radical femininity:

a mighty mildness of repose in swiftness.
                    (*Call Me*, p. 6710)

> ...
> post *naked lunch*
> panislamic
> femininity
>
> penelope's explosive reweaving
> mystic riffs of absence
>
> my soul is a jelly fish, without a womb
> light descends in the gutted out space of the

10 Olson is quoting from *Moby Dick* where the white whale appears for the first time.

dome. (küçük İskender,   *souljam*[11]

That moment when Istanbul reveals herself to Melville as an erotic mystery for the first time was also the moment scales dropped from my eyes. The city described by Melville one hundred and fifty years ago in your book was exactly the city I knew, its street names, its hills, its chaotic and crowded beauty, which has a vertiginous effect on Melville himself. A continuity was established between my life as a writer in the States and my home in Turkey—*between two languages.*

*

Dear Charles,

"Fed/allah[12] [who casts no shadows] was a creature such as civilized, domestic people in the temperate zone only see in their dreams, and then but dimly." (*Moby Dick*)

Your book bursts with hints that it knows more than its author, often quoting from Melville's writings:

"Ahab's larger, darker, deeper part remains unhinted." (*Call Me,* p.54[13])

---

11   Eda: An Anthology, p.310
12   "Allah" is the Islamic/Sufi God.
13   Olson is quoting from *Moby Dick* here.

You devote the last fifth of *Call Me Ishmael* to Melville's descriptions of Constantinople in the journal he kept while he made a pilgrimage to Jerusalem (like "a migrant backtrailing to Asia") after the writing of *Moby Dick*. You sense intensely the potent effect his encounter with the city has on him, reminiscent of his youthful experiences in the Pacific. *But you miss its significance*:

> That Melville did, on this trip, at Constantinople and elsewhere, find some spontaneity towards women suggests a change in the contours of his psyche profound enough to free forces in him long checked. He ranges the polyglot city wildly, writes about it extravagantly. He mixes in the crowds of the suburbs of Galata and Pera. He mounts the bridges to watch them moving below. When he leans over the First Bridge his body is alive as it has not been   since he swung with Jack Chase in maintops above the Pacific. *The difference: he is brooding over a city of a million and a half of human beings, not so many square miles of empty space* [italics my own].[14]

The last sentence is the key for me in this passage. You miss the continuity between the Pacific and Constantinople in Melville's consciousness that *Call Me Ishmael* repeatedly suggests. *What you miss is the*

---

14   *Call Me*, p. 95

submerged, potent drive towards Asia in your own book.
You, Olson the man, turns away from it. You see a
"difference," rather than continuity. As a poet of mid-
twentieth century, your vision's perimeter remains
Western. Ahab's nineteenth century Pacific of whaling
ships metamorphosizes into American space: its
home Gloucester, nestled on the Atlantic, backed by
the American continent, extending into the Pacific.
In your poetics, the Pacific is a western extension (an
American lake).

*Charles, you miss that in your vision also water turns
into land, as in Melville's journals it turns into a city.*
You regard Melville's pilgrimage as a Nietzschean
loss of nerve—as Melville the man's succumbing to
Christianity, reflected according to you in a decline in
his work after *Moby Dick*.
The Mediterranean is the Old World, as opposed
to America the new. This is the way you end *Call Me
Ishmael*:

At the end of the *Paradiso*, when from the
seventh sphere the earth is so small its features are
obscured as the moon's to us, Dante recognizes one
spot on all its surface—that entrance to the West,
the Pillars. Dante's last glance is on the threshold
to that future Columbus made possible.

The third and final Odyssey was Ahab's. The
Atlantic crossed, the new land America known,

the dream's death lay around the Horn, where West returned to East. The Pacific is the end of the UNKNOWN, which Homer's and Dante's Ulysses open men's eyes to. END of individual responsible only to himself. Ahab is the end....

The son of the father of Ocean was a prophet Proteus....[15]

Ahab is not the end. He continues in you. He continues in *Eda*, in Constantinople, the shadow Pillars in the East and what lies beyond.

The journal entries specifically relating to Istanbul occupy about three pages in your book. They are not the focus of your argument. They lie there peripherally, prophetically, a seeds (or virus, depending on one's point of view] to be picked by someone in the future.

Your book bristles with intimations of the future, of an Asiatic new vision, even though you, the person, may not be aware of the direction implications of your sowing.

It is in the seeds you plant that I receive Melville's baton for a reoriented vision turned to the East, a new poetics for our time. An abstract space—made of the ocean of language— opened up in *Eda*.

It is on the mongrel, giddy, transnational, democratic, veiled, erotic city Melville sees one hundred and fifty years ago that I build the third leg of *Eda*, a vision of Istanbul as an elusive, contradictory

---

15   *Call Me*, pp. 118/9.

mistress:

> To the bazaar. A wilderness of traffic. Furniture, arms, silk, confectionary, shoes, sandles— everything. (Cairo). Crowded overhead with stone arches, with side openings.

> Immense crowds. Georgeans, Armenians, Greeks, Jews, & Turks are the merchants. Magnificent embroidered silks & gilt sabres & caparisons for horses.

> You loose yourself & are bewildered & confounded with the labyrinth, the din, the barbaric confusion of it all.

> The Propontis, the Bisphorus, the Golden Horn, the domes, the minarets, the bridges, the men of war, the cypresses. Indescribable.[16]

*

Istanbul, the city of unspeakable beauty; the city of stench, crooked streets, endless vice; the long coveted prize of the Islamic Ottoman Empire; the vulnerable, beloved, cherished spiritual center of Eastern Christianity; the site of the rational, tent-like simplicity of Turkish Imperial architecture [1]; the awesome interior space of the Hagia Sofia; the

---

16   Melville, Journals, quote by Olson in *Call Me Ishmael*, p. 95.

37

European and Asian city; the city of crossings and bridges and double crosses; the city gorgeous to the eye, even more beautiful in its secrets; the city of spiritual yearning and impulse murder; the city of disco bars whose basement forms a Byzantine palace; the city of violet water; the city of trysts; the city where place names gain fetishistic value; the city where life and history are cheap, and they are both everywhere.

The paradoxical nature of Istanbul is the obsessive reference point of 20th century Turkish poetry. Almost no poem is untouched by it -its shape, its street names, its people, objects and activities, its geographic and historical locus. As the city evolves, the poetry responds, trying to re-organize, make sense of the changes. This interplay between city and language resonates spiritually, erotically, politically, philosophically.[17]

Thank you, Charles.

Murat Nemet-Nejat
May, 2015

---

17   *Eda: An Anthology,* p.5.

Claudia Moreno Parsons

Dearest Olson –

FIRST FACT is prologue[1]

The fact is, my letter to you is urgent in the face of AMERICA. How can I describe to you where we have come, and where we have not? This has been a rainy fall, and with winter near it's darker every night. I'm huddling up in my Brooklyn apartment, wondering what you would say if you could see the world.

I take SPACE to be the central fact to man born in America, from Folsom Cave to now. I spell it large because it comes large here. Large, and without mercy.

The fact is, this is a meditation on space. I've been reading *Maximus*, and it makes me think of home. How does home fit into the world, how did it change, who lives there? I've been thinking a lot about the spaces we live in and what we do with them. You said,

Ahab is no democrat

and that he is certainly not. And in America, his power has expanded, his mania and fury and single-mindedness is trying to whip us into obedience to a false democracy. This has been a difficult year, Olson, a year full of violence and sadness and outrage in America, but it is no wonder why.

A political system called "democracy" had led men to think they were "free" of aristocracy.

I was born in Brooklyn. Like Gloucester, it is surrounded by the sea, with bays and inlets filled with boats tethered to their docks. Brooklyn in the twenty-first century has become a brand and a symbol: for wealth, for hip affect and coolness, but I come from a very old part of Brooklyn that still stands on its own, miles from the nearest subway stations. Before any of us got there, the Lenni-Lenape Indians lived there, and they did not share the worldviews that came later. Mill Basin was a small, closed local that seemed to forget it was attached to an outside world, and it harbored its fears close to its heart, growing its hatreds and keeping to itself.

When I was a girl, my family and I walked to the marina out near the end of wide Flatbush Avenue, all the way from our house to Nick's Lobster, a seafood market and fish shop at the mouth of the Belt Parkway, the red and white signal that you have arrived in Mill Basin. We sat on the edge of the water, eating pretzels while we watched the boats in the bay. This was not a fishing village, or a shipping center, though at one time it was some of both. This place became a haven for wealthy Brooklyn families to settle, and they built bigger and bigger houses, each with their own dock. My family and I lived deep on the other side of the water, in a garden apartment on a tree-filled block, and we rented that little apartment in the middle all the homeowners. My mother and I stood apart from those other families, my mother coming from Puerto Rico and married to an Italian American who saved us from the worst of the ostracism because of his light connections – his Italianness, his presumed Catholicness, his mother – to the history of the place. His skin was even darker than hers, though, and he was a bohemian, so our story was one of being outside. Walking along the fences that lined the blocks along the way, keeping us out of the boat slip and rental businesses, I wondered about this life on the water. My family didn't swim or fish or boat, but my parents loved to walk along this water and listen to the seagulls. We would slip in behind the chain link fence at one of its openings to rest and watch, and I remember being wary of this bit of world I didn't know anything about, and I was vaguely worried about possibly trespassing into a space I wasn't sure we were supposed to be.

Flatbush Avenue, that wide main drag that leads in its great length on one end from the Manhattan Bridge – the road to the outside world – and on the other end to the highway leading toward Long Island – the country – was filled with Irish bars and small grocers. I walked with my grandmother from Avenue N, onto Flatbush, all the way to Kings Highway, where the neighborhood changed names and became Flatlands as it continued toward "the city." We stopped for fruit, we went to the bank, we ate pizza at Apollo, where there was an ancient jukebox in the back corner with big, wide push buttons. The owner of Apollo would eventually fall in ruins from a wayward son who blew all of their money on what the neighborhood would call vice and sin, and they judged:

> *"Pardon me, but*
> *what church*
> *do you belong to,*
> *may I ask?"*[2]

I went to those bars when I was no longer a kid, and I feared the men and women inside, because it seemed to me that they forgot that Flatbush Avenue did lead out of itself.

My grandmother and I bought live crabs that were packed into a small crate at the fish market on a corner of Avenue N. We walked the few blocks back to her house, where her husband – a grandfather to me – was waiting to cook them. We were giggling about carrying a box of live crabs, and I was only a little girl then, and partway back to the apartment, the box slipped a little and the crabs started to escape. We scrambled to pick them up and get them back in the box before they could run away, and I thought about how I had seen fishermen's boxes full of crabs on television, and when I was older I learned that Jamaica Bay was a place where crabs were abundant, and these crabs that my grandmother bought were from the local waters.

My family and I also used to take walks along what we called "the lake" but which is actually a salt marsh. We picked up bagels with butter and potato chips and iced teas at the big deli on Flatbush Avenue and continued our walk into the next neighborhood over, Marine Park, winding our way down the path along the marsh. It was wild and mostly untended in those years, and we felt secluded and adventurous. My parents drank their *café con leche* out of their red and black checkered thermos, and we sat on an old blanket on the sand. I realize now that my parents were searching for an old, wild Brooklyn that existed at the edges of and just below the surfaces of this suburbanized Brooklyn that we never really fit into. I only half knew at the time that our family was different in our undertaking of these adventures, this search for something older and wilder than what sat on the surface. It is striking to me now, that we had sacrificed a certain level of normalcy, and that we had done it deliberately.

Mill Basin never became the busy shipping center the Dutch settlers had hoped it would be, and it turned residential very early on. At one time this part of Brooklyn had been filled with salt marshes like the one we hiked along, but the big industrial companies that began settling in the late nineteenth century filled them in to create dry docks and bring workers, which it did by the thousands. Mill Basin never became part of the outside in a real way in part because the rail system never reached it. Isolated Mill Island was too far even then to be thought of as vital to the rest of the city, and the neighborhood remained on its own. By the 1960s, industry was vanishing and the suburbs, its blocks filled with two-story brick houses and two-story aluminum siding, stoops and porches and walk-in apartments fronted by driveways and cement sidewalks, were installed. My grandmother came out to the neighborhood in 1965 with her husband and a truck full of heavy oak furniture and my parents followed them in 1970, chased out of Manhattan by high rents and small spaces and landlords who didn't want to rent their apartments to anyone who owned a piano, which my father did.

Mill Basin hasn't changed a lot since I was a girl. The supermarket goods have grown more international as immigrants from the Caribbean began moving in, and I know that my mother is happy to find the food she wants to cook closer to home. But what does it mean, how does a space get MADE, when you are so far from everything else? The only ways out of the place are by car or bus – the subway station is too far to walk to, leaving a sense of enclosure or being trapped. This is not hip Brooklyn: it is deeply disconnected from the world's image of this New York City borough in the twenty-first century. I left Mill Basin behind, but my parents stayed, and eventually the neighborhood grew into them and they grew into the little world around them.

When I imagine your walks along the streets of Gloucester, I imagine your body and your voice, and the ways you made into poetry the things you saw and the people you spoke to. You remain in Gloucester, and I wonder if my family will remain in Mill Basin after everyone has left for good. How do voices remain?

How do spaces resonate with our lives?

LAST ACT

You aren't here to see this, Olson, so bear with me while I scream for a moment.

The fact is, this is also a meditation on violence. This space in the years since you were writing and thinking about it has grown denser, and our problems always more pressing.

Because it is America, all of her space, the malice, the root.

NUMBERS: We have continued to maim, murder, and destroy our women, men, and children, all over the American continent. Untold numbers of missing in Mexico (the fault indirectly and directly of AMERICAN intervention and years of historical fuckery). A frightening number of cities with frighteningly militarized police forces. (And when I say militarized, I mean MILITARIZED, Olson, levels of force that would slay your capacity for reason. How do we get ourselves out of this one?)

Olson, we lost Amiri (to you, though, he must remain LeRoi, I know).[3] If he had lived, he would not have been surprised. He saw the policing, the mass incarcerations, the racist and classist horrors. Would these things, the newest ones, have put him over the edge? Probably not, but how his heart would have been

45

broken, again. We are lost people, and he knew that. I'm turning to you for a little hope and reassurance, Olson. Why do we continue to fail? Amiri wrote to Ed[4] many years ago, and he was fretting because you had written to him, and you were concerned about his social attitudes, &c., baiting him, he said. Amiri's ideas about violence, you weren't so sure if you wholly agreed. I am not so sure I wholly agree either, but this is a complicated business, toppling the *aristocracy*. There is a barbarism at work that is trying to take over the whole SPACE of the place, and in places and times that seem to come more and more quickly, that barbarity wins. The answer? Ah, Olson, that is the question. Right now, America has taken to the streets, it is demanding answers and disrupting things as they are, trying to wake and move and break it all open, and the authorities are resisting. You saw this before, and I wonder, would you be surprised to see it yet again? Like Amiri, probably not.

> *(1) democracy ha[s] not rid itself of overlords; (2) the common man, however free, leans on a leader, the leader, however dedicated, leans on a straw.*

What is this American project? There is deep skepticism, and yet, it is profound, and there is brilliance in all this ugliness. What I want to know is, how can we see the apparatus, the workings that lay underneath and that maybe will get us somewhere? You say that the local is the prism through which we understand the cosmos. In Brooklyn these days, the streets are a whirlwind of voices and bodies demanding a true America. Do you remember that final line to Amiri? You said,

> *Ok Not at all to argue. Solely to try to get in there*
> *where in fact I feel completely free too and want*
> *to get back to you with, love, Charles*[5]

I want to end this letter on that note, with love, because that is my style too, the thing I feel most and want the most. That is the human spirit – I know you believed in this, and I stand with you.

   With love, your constant reader,
   Claudia

1. All quotes from *Call Me Ishmael*, unless otherwise noted.
2. *Maximus, to Gloucester, Letter 19 (A Pastoral Letter)*
3. Amiri Baraka, formerly LeRoi Jones (1934 – 2104)
4. Edward Dorn (1929 – 1999)
5. Letter from Olson to LeRoi Jones, 1964

Susan Thackrey

excerpt from
Henry Ferrini's film, *Polis is This*:

He wanted always to get back to the beginning because he really felt that it was only there that any change was possible.

And, if you're talking about political change, that that's the only possible way of changing form, of changing consciousness, of changing the uses of power – and, specifically, I think, human masculine power, since that's the way it's been manifested since Homer. And, as he would see it, since Zeus took over and buried the Titans underground...and Olson considered himself a Titan...

I had an amazing dream about Charles. I was visiting Cairo. I was out back *behind* the museum and it was daytime, but then suddenly it was night, and he came up behind me and he said "look up" and I looked up and he said "so you can see the *whole* hypostasis" and when I looked up, instead of seeing the constellations, I saw the forms that lay behind the constellations. That's Charles – It is in the night...It is and it's not the forms we're used to seeing and the ones that give us comfort. It's something else...

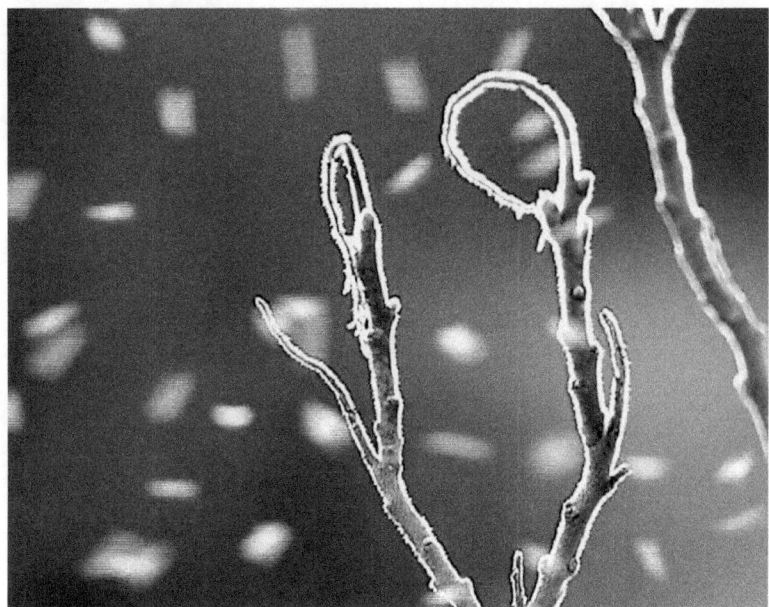

Alana Siegel

Dear Charles,

This letter is one of thanks. As I am writing to you, I am searching my memory, for how I came to your work initially, and what your work gave me. I am trying to think of what I learned from you. We never knew each other directly, but I do know a student of yours—Charles Stein. It was through him, or simultaneous to meeting him, I discovered your work at Bard College.

It seems so far away now, the liberation you gave me. I remember my teacher, Robert Kelly, urging me to read "Projective Verse." The essay was in a book at the library at school—nothing special looking—it was one of those *library books* with a bland tan cover—hard, and minisculely pebbled. I remember reading "Projective Verse" and thinking to myself that the way you spoke, what sounded like slang, was no longer slang, and the awkwardness of this from Shakespeare to—how old does slang go?—and the next generation, and the generation after that witnessing the voice of a person in the past *sounding cool* and how that coolness doesn't last, yet still remains close, in an unexplored translation of the anchors of eternal youth—(yesterday a friend of mine was auditioning for a theater company, and she was nervous because she was not, as she described, a "Shakespeare robot," but I encouraged her to audition, and added that isn't it strange how in

Shakespeare the emotion endures, but the language has changed—and what does this reveal about the nature of emotion, and the nature of language, and their resonant and dissonant evolutions through time—does emotion change? And if it does, how do we have record of it? Language no doubt changes, which accounts for all of the languages that have died, and continue to die, and continue to change—so I said to her, or asked, "Why isn't the curious space between the speech of Shakespeare as being no longer connected to the colloquial, but the emotion, recognizable—why isn't the chasm in between the authentic emotion and the no longer authentic speech (speech existing only in the theatrical, only in the literary) why isn't this space more deeply explored, more than polishing, coaxing actors and actresses into becoming "Shakespeare robots," as a sort of triumph of theatrical sensibility?—

I was in the library, going to school, inside a formality, which feels so far from me now. It was not only that I giggled around your changed spelling of words or how you abbreviated some of them, as well as well known writers—how could you be so casual, so comfortable in this history of those before you? I thought to myself, in awe of this giant habitation. When I first read "Projective Verse," I thought I knew what you meant, but I wasn't quite sure. I read it again, and maybe a third time. The pages were yellow, and like I said, the book itself, the cover, was bland—was not the original. Then suddenly a landscape opened—it was the realization of the possibilities of movement you were transmitting—the zig-zag of it—it was rabid, shocking, heretical even, to the ways in which I comported myself, organized my thought in the various discourses I was introduced to in school. It dawned on me that I had been in school my whole life. School itself was an organization of knowledge, so of thought. You were handing over to me, as I saw it, as you write in Maximus, "a metal hot from boiling water," and it was here that I began to feel the frightening aspect of the Muses, the Sphinxes, the everlasting orders that are of this art called Poetry, at its root, and in its most exposed and secret precincts—it was how you stutteringly called, curled, slammed, wrestled to convey this glittering, this fish escaping, the photons shaking—that the poem was a body that a dancer has to warm—"how to dance sitting down," you wrote. Isn't that the question? Like "Anxiety of Influence" but something different from it. "Dakinis" are sometimes translated as "sky dancers," other times as "destabilizing energies." Robert Duncan, in "The Opening of the Field," quotes St. John of Ephesus in saying, "He who misses the Dance, mistakes the event." Or how you focus on Heisenberg, and the impossibility of measuring anything, or having to stop motion to measure matter's mass, thus distorting it, thus returning to an older science, of having to kill the body in order to study its parts. I think of Athanasius Kircher and his revered madness of mind. How Champollion says later that the way in which he translated the hieroglyphs was wrong—and I want to know why he says he was wrong. Is it possible to translate writing wrong? I'm not being post-modern about this. I'm thinking about this, and the authority every person continues to shuck from themselves with letting certain people be translators, and others not. It's like Giambattista Vico, when he says that in Rome, only the wealthy were permitted to perform divination—I think about this today, with the privatization of language learning, and specialized study—that the act of divining, is the hands in the pot free form approachable flesh of mind you write yourself—that writing is no special act other than this action, this activeness, as you write in "The Special View of History," that "man must do something about himself," and "history is to do."

I think of the image in the poem by Parmenides, where the goddess lends out her hand, and with a chariot, being offered says, these horses will take you as far as you wish to go. And I quoted you in my first book of poetry, from "The Special View of History," when you write, "My memory is the history of time." That did something to me. I mean it really did something to me. I wonder what you would have to say now about the scientific research of parallel worlds, of "the multiverse." The research still exists in this realm which is not "scientifically confirmed" and people joke about it, because it sounds more like "science fiction" than "science," but it was this kind of thinking, this possibility of travel, mental and physical, which your work brought me to. I was excited by the mind. I came to be. A teacher of mine said to me once, "You must fall in love with attention." I keep on thinking of the story of Cupid and Psyche as emblematic of this wild dance of mind and thought and form, some people choose to not even experience, because you don't have to. I think you say elsewhere in TSVH, "History is to want to."

I'm looking to my right, and I see the declining light of the afternoon shining on my metal ruler that says "non-skid" and additionally, the brand name is "HELIX." I think of the physicality you were calling for in poetry, and sometimes I wonder why you didn't become a dancer. In the past few months, I have been moving away from the act of writing, as I have been further drawn to what I am calling "performance." Sometimes I say to myself that this is a development of poetry—it is what poetry wants, what it is moving towards—am I just deflecting this action of writing, trying to override it, trying to get away from this untameable thrashing of mind, that I can think anything, that what I think is arbitrary, and the language in me, can be totally re-arranged—I feel the ghost of it like the town my grandfather grew up in— remnants of trauma—the language wants to be born again, incessantly so—when with my grandfather in his car driving home, he asked, "Do you know what we're driving on?" He added, "A fiery ball with a thin skin upon which nuclear reactions are happening constantly." He was speaking of the earth. He was a mechanic.

I am asking for an older art, where the science my

grandfather was schooled in, the physics, finds its older belonging. It's why someone like myself is accused of having no discipline. I want to say it's something else, this endless turning about, around, this unbridled curiosity in how things have come to be, of needing to seek origins, of everything being the past.

I think of Jaime d'Angulo, and listened to Andrew Schelling speak of him a couple months ago. As I walked out of his lecture, I thought to myself, that this is what you were after—the Tower of Babel is what you are close to—the Titans—why you spoke of them—you must have known what it's like to have a hundred heads, a hundred tongues, to be a hydra—this is how I feel—it's a madness—it's a resistance and it's a complete surrender, surrounding—a skull like a planet and many moons orbiting the eyes—it's unavoidable—or it's the void that won't stop not being the void—it's beautiful and then it's—how Picasso described what he thought was the most beautiful woman—in profile she was beautiful, and then she turns her face, and she is the ugliest woman you have ever seen.

I stared at my face in the mirror this morning, trying to re-create the face of the woman who sat next to me in a restaurant last week. She could have sat anywhere else, but she chose to sit next to me—why? She scowled at me, then began to talk on her phone. She needed nothing from me. I tried to re-create her face today, and the emotion within her—because I am initiating a class called "DOING," largely inspired by the work of the Polish director Grotowski, where I want the human body to become a glyph. I want the human body to be like Taliesin, singing of all the people and things he was in so many lives, and now a bard. I want the body to be an ever changing form, to experience through itself all the objects of its attention. I feel like you were after this, going towards it, when you write in "Human Universe," "My assumption is, that the contemporary Maya are what they are because once there was a concept at work which kept attention so poised that (1) men were able to stay so interested in the expression and gesture of all creatures, including at least three planets in addition to the human face, eyes and hands, that they invented a system of written record, now called hieroglyphs, which, on its very face, is verse, the signs were so clearly and densely chosen that, cut in stone, they retain the power of the objects of which they are the images....."

This may or may not have been true of the Mayans, and how will we ultimately know if this was so? But what you are able to imagine from what you saw, the possibility that this was true, points to, shoulders, a capacity of mind, an ongoing attention, which you recognize is lost, and you're projecting, you're feeling for, another place and time, where these powers of mind were just-how-it-was. It is this imagination of mind, which I now understand in Projective Verse, and am honest with my impulses of thinking another place and time was a certain way, and knowing, the impossibility of ever being able to recover the moment that passes—the Greek words for the differences in these kinds of time—is it the kairos, or another word, for the moment that keeps cutting itself away, drawing closer and equally far. Sometimes I have wondered if your massive map, just as Ezra Pound created his—of the maxim "all times are contemporaneous in the mind" does that mean not in the body—are you indulging that dualism? Or in this statement of Pound's, does the mind include the body, and all times are simply contemporaneous, and we have to seek out the glamours, the illusions of other moments, others nows, to reveal the illusion of our own?

I see Jaime d'Angulo again, and he is, as he was described to me, without any recording instrument. He is sitting, a stirring form, with ears and eyes wide open, avidly listening. He is taking all the world in, of the language he doesn't know. He knows he has to translate it, and this translation will be like a kind of money that isn't coined. It will be the kind of kairos, what you receive from the phenomenal world at large, at small, when you dare to let your body be an instrument, to so awkwardly hum and receive and transmit the mystery of matter—he, like an angel, new to the world, as anyone is, when so relieved, so inspired, whatever verbs give way to the romance which so easily could be a horror—I think of the lines of yours, "I'm going to hate to leave this earthly Paradise," and I think of Jerome Rothenberg, who was in my dream the other night, and what message he came with, I still have not fully deciphered, and I think of my friend Katy Bohinc, whose book I just read, and how it said to me, so many things, but one of them was what it's like to be in love with the mind, and that means you are in love with someone, but it's not that simple. It's like a dream I had once, which I include below. Apologies if this letter has gone on too long, or is not so properly composed, but I wanted to write with what first came to mind, and I had the feeling that you would give ear to it more than if it was heavily wrought.

My regards, thank you again, and dream below,

Alana

THREE MESSENGERS

It is not that they are my lovers, nor that I am their beloved, but each has come to me. Our eyes hold us to each other, while the space between our bodies, suspends us from each other.

One of the messengers is a boy I knew when younger, who was painfully obese. Later, after having lost touch with him, he became a celebrity, seemingly loved by the world, by his fame. Now in dream he stands alone, in the light shadows of his trailer. He has lost much of his weight now—and there he stands—our blue eyes meet—he hands me a text of Ibn Arabi.

Later, I am meeting with Peter Lamborn Wilson. We are sitting at a picnic table with other people. I feel a sense of sanctity marked by a movement underneath the table coming toward me. I am apprehending, anticipating, embracing what is soon to appear, then suddenly before me is a gift Peter is giving.

It is an original text of Ibn Arabi, written in Persian. I can feel the weight of the age of the text and the weight of Peter's head, bowing. Or perhaps the weight of his head is shading his heart, a hyena or a hummingbird, so wild yet so light, so defenseless—a tiny, utterly effusive offering—he shadows. The vigil of his head becomes his words, a solace marked by balance. The weight of his head gives us time, gives us text.

With his head still lowered, he hands the text to me. The text has a French title, possibly written by Henry Corbin, sounding like, "Symbologique". I feel a deep love but I am not so confused as to think I love "Peter"—It is clear to me it is the moment that loves us.

A third messenger who might have been the first has also come with a text of Ibn Arabi. I am aware this is becoming a theme. Each messenger arrives in all the splendor of the beloved. The feeling in my chest canopies a resplendence, arches the heat of our hearts above our heads.

But it is known to me. It is not through the body that their soul will meet my own. One messenger is only a friend, while another was obese and grotesque. What each brings is an emotion I recognize as what romantic love in the past has come to give, but now, the text is what is given. The face of each man is lowered, hands held up. The text is held up. It overcomes us. It is without us. It is what makes us meet. This child that does not need us. This soul that divides us, and is divided from us, distances our bodies, yet holds us, momentarily, by the grace we see, in our eyes unspoken.

Tom Cheetham

Dear Charles,

Hope you don't mind getting a letter out of the blue. We have a common interest. You were one of the first people over here to really *use* Henry Corbin's work and I have spent a long time thinking about him. I did a bit of poking around and found that it was poets who took him most to heart. You folks, along with the Eranos crowd. Most of his colleagues never knew what to make of him. But poets did. Which makes perfect sense. You all took his stuff and ran with it. I saw your library and I love the scrawls you left in the margins of his books — "Wow! Wow!" Your enthusiasm was at least as great as mine. And deeper, more informed. You weren't puzzled by him, as I was for quite a while. But I was coming from a very different place. For you, and even more for Duncan, Corbin was a natural ally, just operating in a different universe. That knotted, dense and difficult essay on cyclical time that you read first was a great place to start — it has pretty much everything in it. Worlds upon Worlds. It's far from the most elegant thing he ever wrote but you went right to the heart of it. A little time with Maud and Butterick and I found that not long after you turned loose "Maximus, at the Harbor." You already had the middle voice thing from Wolpe at Black Mountain who said it's what makes music work — which is an exquisite thing to say — and extremely Corbinian. His vision is founded on harmony and the musical structure of the cosmos. For this and a host of other reasons you were primed and ready for the *apophainesthai!* that beats powerfully right at the center of Corbin's cosmos. But oh my! How it explodes at the harbor! Okeanos rages, men rape, the Great Ocean is angry, and wants the Perfect Child...

So much of the vocabulary of this sudden, intense storm comes direct from Corbin. But emerging from long immersion in his work I was knocked back on my heels when I read it. Poor Henry was shocked by what Hillman and his colleagues later on did with his careful neologism, the *mundus imaginalis*, the *imaginal* world, and warned them against misusing it in contexts ripped free of their moorings (he should have expected it, and he's a pretty notorious borrower himself). He certainly didn't know of your work, but if he'd read this!? He'd have been utterly dismayed and would have pointed out to you, as he implicitly did to Hillman, the demonic possibilities he warns of on those very same pages you quote from — the soul's "demonic virtualities" which lead so easily to the abyss. He would have thought it the same kind of mis-step that lead to Nietzsche's "failed initiation;" the same sort of failure that he saw in Hillman's unwillingness to reject pathology, and in Jung's desire to attain a wholeness which somehow includes the Shadow, rather than rejecting it utterly. He thought they all shared an inability to distinguish among kinds of darkness. There is a divine darkness "at the approach to the Pole" and there are demonic darknesses of evil. The imaginal, he said, is not innocuous. I've learned a lot from Jung, I'm a great fan of Hillman, and I'm perfectly willing to use Corbin's work in ways he wouldn't have approved of, so I'm not being critical — but I'm wondering if you know just how far you pushed the envelope of his mystical psychocosmology? I've been interested by this kind of tension, between Corbin and Hillman in particular, for a long time. It seems to me now not *primarily* an argument about the role of Imagination or even of the nature of the *imaginal* (though it is that too), but rather about the role of darkness itself. Or darknesses. For the Zoroastrians this world is a realm of Mixture — particles of light embedded in darkness. Corbin's only interest is in the escape of the particles of Light. He's a spokesman for a Gnostic — Zoroastrian — Platonic — Judaic — Christian — Islamic metacosmogony of salvation and flight of the Light from Darkness. It's a "gothic cosmology" of ascent towards Heaven. Right from the beginning I've been wary of his tendency to disappear into the Beyond. What if you're more interested in physical bodies than in subtle ones? He thought the doctrine of the Incarnation was a catastrophic mistake, for reasons that seem to me cogent and important and completely in line with his love of Islamic mysticism, but that refusal does have consequences. What if the dense particles of matter and their accompanying darknesses seem worth attending to? Does this make us demons? No. Is it potentially dangerous? Everything is dangerous. Is it essentially human? Sure. The passage through the world is more difficult than the passage beyond. You and Corbin both have quite a vertical thrust. But somehow you're moving in different directions and the energy is different — which shows how simplistic and misleading the whole vertical/horizontal thing really is. It seems to me that if you stood together in front of Bernini's St. Teresa you'd be in rather different places. As Corbin insists, the fundamental fact of alchemy is that your mode of knowledge depends upon your mode of being. Yours and his are, I am pretty sure, distinct.

While I was ferreting out your use of Corbin, I was looking at Duncan too. My first and lasting impression was that with him the natural affinities are closer. You just have to read the HD Book to see that. The first poem that jumped out at me dates from a few years before "Maximus, at the Harbor," and it must have been written before he read any Corbin. It struck me when I first read it as about as perfect a one page outline of Corbin's world as I could imagine. "Often I am Permitted to Return to a Meadow" has no rage, no rape, no anger. It has "flowers" that are "flames lit to the Lady", who is "Queen Under The Hill" and "whose hosts are a disturbance of words within words." The "meadow is a place of first permission, / everlasting omen of what is." It feels to me every time I read it that here we're in the imaginal world as Corbin knew it. But your meeting with Corbin at the harbor is a far more interesting encounter. Rage of ocean without a shore.

You devoured the cyclical time essay and the Avicenna book with speed and enthusiasm but nothing else was available in English then. We've got a wider view of him now in English. His work is extremely complex and wide ranging, but it wouldn't be wrong to call him a highly eclectic, wholly ecumenical, post-Islamic Christian mystic and Neo-Platonic theologian with a sensibility based in a medieval vision of angelic hierarchies. You saw that much I am sure. He was no fan of the modern secular world. He was no fan of most modern art and literature, though he had a special fondness for Rilke. In some respects he was a radical liberal, in others a reactionary conservative. He was above all a champion of the central place of Imagination in human life and as a fundamental principle of Creation. The range of his vision makes it possible, and profitable, to read him in a lot of ways. But as he got older and his work became an important source for his relatively few admirers, he worried about what he had unleashed. He thought they were confusing the *imaginal* with the merely imaginary. He warned urgently that the problem was secularization, which resulted in the triumph of "the fantastic, the horrible, the monstrous, the macabre, the miserable and the absurd." In stark contrast, "the art and imagination of Islamic culture in its traditional form are characterized by the hieratic and the serious, by gravity, stylization and meaning." He would have said the same of the art of medieval Christianity. The secularization that spread through western Europe and, soon enough the world, established a realm of the human walled off from that of the Angels, and he had no intention of living there. In the traditional cultures he defends, there is no secular realm in our sense. In those "mythic" cultures there is no wall. There are struggles with the demonic aplenty but Corbin thought at least the stakes were clear and the Orientation towards the Light well-defined. It is otherwise in the secular world, where dis-orientation is the norm and the threat from the darkness often unacknowledged. It seems to me that his critiques of Jung and Hillman, and by extension, of you, are based not on his worries about the secular, but on the question of disorientation. Because you and Jung and Hillman are all engaged in a project to re-establish a mythic cosmology which absorbs the secular inside a wider cosmology. But for Corbin the *disorientation* remains because of your common desire to give the imagination unrestricted access to *everything*. I think that for Corbin, though imagination is in all things and we participate in the energy that is the divine Imagination, the crucial distinction here is between the "imaginary" which is of human origin and contaminated with darkness, and the *imaginal* which gives real knowledge, gnosis, and comes from divine illumination. The *imaginal world* can't be entered, he says, "by housebreaking."

This kind of distinction is at the heart of the difference between Revealed Truth and the contaminated stuff we just "make up." It provides the rationale for the institutionalization of religions everywhere. *But*, and here's the subtle thing, you find in Corbin a profound resistance to institutional, clerical and dogmatic religion. His religion of the imagination is far more Protestant than Catholic, far more individual than institutional, far more liberal than conservative in almost every theological sense. He is the ultimate champion of religious freedom and liberty in the face of dogma and authoritarianism. He did *not* think that secularization necessarily accompanies the breakdown of the Church as guarantor of the Truth. The rise of the secular occurred not because authority broke down but because the Imagination, which is the basis for gnosis and gives access to the divine, was abandoned in favor of secular, agnostic rationality. Secularization spreads when we lose contact with the Angels. But those angels are sources of illumination — they are to our eyes beings of light. And this is one reason appropriation, like Hillman's and yours, is so interesting. It highlights a whole range of questions.

Are we passive receivers of the Word? Or are we participants in its creation? There are times when Corbin clearly has us as absolutely necessary participants. At other times we are only mirrors. I suspect that this may be a persistent tension in his work. No priest, no worldly power can tell you the meaning of the Word — you must find your own hermeneutic Angel. If and when you do then you are the only sure hermeneut of your own Text. But what about while you're seeking? I don't think he meant that we're participants *until* we become mirrors. It's more subtle than that, and for another letter. Sometimes I do wonder if I understand Corbin at all. In any case elsewhere he enthusiastically endorses Schleiermacher's idea that any book written with the same power as the Bible should be included as Scripture. But then he's got a puzzle. He means to include the Qur'an, the Avesta, and the other traditional scriptures of the world. But does he include Goethe? Rilke? Shakespeare? Blake? *Maximus*? And what practical criteria can there be to distinguish fantasy from *vera imaginatio* for those of us who live outside a traditional culture? There certainly can be no dogmatic, institutional criteria — no Laws. On this he is crystal clear. But how then are we to know? It's up to each of us the discover our own revealed truth — but never to impose it on anyone else. Personally, I'm on Blake's side when he writes "Everything possible to be believed is an image of the truth." For all his eclecticism and hermeneutic liberality, to Corbin such a claim seemed dangerous. I much prefer Corbin the radical hermeneut to the old man worried about his acolytes and his legacy. I get from Corbin, as Hillman did, a passionate embrace of imagination and a willingness to transgress boundaries, and I have found his vision to be transformative and life-affirming. He thought that what had gone wrong with Western civilization was precisely that the Imagination had been abandoned and "left to the poets" and he wanted to retrieve it from you all and expand its range to cover, I think, everything. This seems to me wholly glorious.

I have to say that when I first read your stuff I was not only startled by what you did with Corbin, but also put off by your evident "American-ness" — the grandiosity and expanse of your vision. I thought, well that's fine, but it reminds me too much of my own, hopefully now expunged, longing for a Theory of Everything. The extent of your reach is so GRAND that it worried me. But eventually I realized that you're of course not Theorizing. Rasula says we can't understand *Maximus* unless we see Gloucester as Hurqualya. That shifts everything. He must be right. And in fact this kind of move can anchor Corbin, who was so invested in the Elsewhere as to risk floating off to heaven with the least breeze. Isfahan as an earthly Hurqualya, sure... but oh dear, not *Gloucester* for heavens' sake! To admit Gloucester you certainly can't have a wall between the secular and the sacred — you have to live inside the all-encompassing range of the *mythic*, where impure souls live — the world of *mixture*. But the question is, can you *live* in Gloucester and invoke Corbin's Angels, or will they insist on hauling you off to Heaven? Like you and Hillman, I want *this* world, the world of Gloucester and Atlantic City, and I want the Angels too. I suppose that's what's good about the hierarchy — we can have the basement-level Angels because they're denser and darker and they don't fly so very high. But still they do illuminate the world.

One more thought that seems pertinent. Corbin's mystical sensibility left him a poor judge of the political aspects of the spiritualities he outlined. Corbin once quipped that while the French Leftists of the 60s were in thrall to an ideology of perpetual Revolution, he was proposing something far more profound, a real source of freedom: a perpetual hermeneutics. Hillman thinks his focus on Imagination is both political and revolutionary — and I sometimes wonder if there is really much difference between perpetual revolution and perpetual hermeneutics — maybe they amount to the same thing. And it may be that I'm making too much here of Corbin's vertical thrust and his desire for transcendence and not adequately fleshing out his cosmology — which you certainly wanted to do.

In any case the soul is indeed an onslaught. Corbin was trying to get beyond that — I think he did. I think he lived in that opened field, tending flowers Who are flames lit to the Lady. But maybe most of us can't get there. Maybe most of us live in the chaos, outside the bounds of the place of first permission, where Okeanos rages, forever wanting that Perfect Child.

Hope you are as well as can be expected. I'd love to hear anything you might have to say on any of this. I know it's a knotted tangle. I've been interpreting Corbin for a long time and what I'm trying here is the outline of yet another hermeneutic act — I don't really have the interest, or the need, to pursue it. I got the freedom I'd been longing for all my life from his work and am immensely grateful to him for leaving such a treasure. Oh, one more thing though: Maud said you told him "Maximus at the Harbor" was a "sucker poem," too personal, too subjective, but that nonetheless it shouldn't be dismissed, which is why you left it in. What the hell did you mean? It's clearly very relevant.

Yrs,

Tom Cheetham

Cole Heinowitz

LETTER TO CHARLES OLSON

May 1, 2015
<u>A Poem</u>

You cut into story the primary equal of its parts,
of what has been converted from legend & myth
into something called *history* / where people
having lived here for millennia unrelieved
more or less escapes the conversation.

You know the diminishment I mean,
the present loss of context & the misery
of expenditure & gain—for which read URGENCY
What is it with this country that will not wait
a minute before it strikes
but is always looking for its *history*
as a transcript of experience which
doesn't have what this or that girl said
or did. And this is loss.

Anyone who would try to make this reappear as art
has to damn well respect the consequences,
to make them clear, to compose his refusal of the
miseryin abundance, to walk in that world
where you find the real in any direction
not the spent presentation of some American event
lifting up meaning only to break it on the floor

asserting it should have been realism.

*

Dear Charles,

I'm not going to write to you from my usual position of giving reasons for not writing to assure you I'm alive. Because today is good. The old voices I've neglected have come back and are demanding an outlet with surprising kindness given the criminals they've had to live with.

Anyway, I dreamt last night about your vision of the beautiful boat. But either my memory failed or my eyesight did & I realized I'd have to build the thing entirely from scratch. At first I froze, then suddenly the boat tacked & I was jumping sideways to avoid being hit by the boom. I was reading this in a book I could see but couldn't feel. When I went to turn the page my fingers didn't touch anything. It was the Sacred Book of Language. It was open to a page that read

Work dexterously with delight.
Draw everything out from your heart.
Meet it with your mind.
Compose the pieces.
Make them adjust.

There was something throbbing in my heart, dark with a red glow, spreading into my guts & throat. I wanted it to spread through my limbs & radiate out of my body but I only knew how to draw the forces *in*. So I gathered it back to my heart & rocked it like a baby. Someone on my left was beating the air away from my head with a feather. The shapes of an eagle & then a butterfly appeared in a fierce red glow. They drew closer & closer until all I could see was the color.

Steorra / star from a bird's wing...

*

A Myth

Back when human language was an animal, it carried the earth & the sky in its mouth & everything spoke. That was when the sun fell in love with the moon. Sun had heard that Moon was contained in an old hollow log, so he scooped out the log to build a boat that would carry them away.

Foolish Sun,
Swelling Sun,
Lie quiet, Moon is missing
& only Deer can bring her back.
Lie quiet, Sun,
& wait for Deer to pass—
For nothing lasts.

So Sun waited the entire day & when night finally

came, Moon appeared in the sky. Sun stole a deerskin to disguise himself & flew to her & they were joined. Moon shone brightly then, but soon she went in search of other lovers. And the more she loved the more brightly she shone. She grew so bright that no living thing on earth could sleep & everyone went mad. They begged Sun to put out one of her eyes. And, because Sun was jealous of Moon's lovers, he did.

*

Dear Charles,

This morning someone told me that the Weathermen split from SDS & became terrorists because they were brainwashed by a cult. He remembered being at what he thought was a party when he realized that everyone was performing a ritual & that they wanted him to join. For several minutes, he felt the blackest guilt for all the Beings he had harmed, willingly or not. Then all of a sudden the guilt disappeared & in every cell he felt his oneness with the universe.

Since I knew you studied Crowley, I thought: Now is the time to write to Olson & tell him why I've been silent so long. He will understand.

This is a ritual to banish silences.

Love,
        Cole

Jeff Gardiner

The Mytho—[1]

During his years at Black Mountain College, Charles Olson delivered three extended series of lectures that were prospective of his work to come: *The Chiasma, or, Lectures in the New Sciences of Man* (March 1953), lectures on Shakespeare (1954), and *The Special View of History* (1956). These lectures were groundwork for Olson's later writing, lectures, and teaching. All of these lectures were prospective of work to come...sometimes considerably later in his writing. For instance, while working on the material that became his lectures on the new sciences of man, one sees little crossover of that material into his poetry. While working on the lectures, he simultaneously proofs newly published poems and continues writing *Maximus* poems. Only considerably later does one see variations of many of the ideas first explored in *The Chiasma* lectures in his classes and talks at Buffalo in the early 60s, the 1965 conferences in Vancouver and Berkeley, particularly the Berkeley talk published by Donald Allen titled *Causal Mythology*, his lecture on *Poetry and Truth* at Beloit College (1968), his last lectures in 1969 at the

---

1   This essay was originally delivered at the conference Re-Viewing Black Mountain College 2, October 8-10, 2010, hosted by the Black Mountain College Museum and Art Center at University of North Carolina, Asheville.

University of Connecticut, and a number of *Maximus* poems written throughout the 1960s.

Of his three major Black Mountain series, *The Chiasma: Lectures in the New Sciences of Man* best shows the broad range of Olson's thought.

In these lectures, he moves from Cro-Magnon man's cave art to then recent scholarship in geography, biology, archaeology, and mythology. (The inclusion of the latter as a science was due to his reading of Carl Jung's and Karl Kerenyi's recently translated *Essays on the Science of Mythology*). His attention to each of those sciences is on their methods for reaching back to human origins and their findings in that regard. Although he connects all four of those sciences in his lectures, my talk focuses primarily on mythology, which Olson then regarded as "the ultimate science (at least the crucial 'human' science...the ultimate science of man)." (65)

Throughout *The Chiasma* lectures, Olson takes great care to define his terms, drawing directly from definitions in *Webster's Collegiate Dictionary* and *The Shorter Oxford English Dictionary*. Among the terms he defines are epic, kinetics, life, soul, generate, image, etymology, and the term he spends the most time defining: mythology. In his lecture of March 4, 1953, Olson first looks at the definition of mythology in *Webster's*, which defined it as "a story...to explain some practice, belief, institution, or natural phenomenon," and, following Jung's lead, he rejects that definition, finding instead one that matches his experience of myth in the work of the classicist, J. A. K. Thomson. About Thomson, Olson says, he "is the only source of clarity & exactitude I know—the single one." (63) Thomson presents the etymology of mythology as "TO SPEAK (legein) of WHAT IS SAID (mythos)" (62). Moving the term to the mouth and the act of telling appealed immediately to an inveterate talker and omnivore like Olson.

But Thomson's etymology provides only the starting point for the definition Olson presents in *The Chiasma* lectures. To go beyond etymology, he mines *Essays on the Science of Mythology*. He draws from Kerenyi quoting Bronislaw Malinowski. Malinowski states that "myth in a primitive society...is not a mere tale told but a reality lived." Malinowski asserts that myths are a re-arising of primordial reality and they are not intended to address as Kerenyi states a "non-existent 'desire to explain.'" (Jung and Kerenyi, 6) This latter phrase Olson picks up, varies, and extends throughout his lectures. He first elides it with his own insistence that at root mythology is experience and experience is the base of knowing. Olson adds:

> there is no desire to explain—there is solely the desire to experience, & vice versa: to experience is to know (histor). That is, *to tell about it, and to tell about it as others have told it*, is one act, simply, that the reality is one, now, & then. (64)

These incidences persist throughout Olson's work

and intensify in the last years of his life. The "desire to experience" becomes pervasive impulse in his later work and life. And he couples experiencing with telling. Olson insists that the crucial characteristic of telling is that it is to re-enact, to make present, and to experience. Following Malinowski, he says of myth that it is "the re-arising of a primordial reality in narrative form...narrative itself is the reality which is original, greater & more important now." (64).

In 1956, in his final Black Mountain lectures, *The Special View of History*, Olson combines Thomson's etymology of mythology with Malinowski's description, saying that "It was not mere word or even an expression of human experience so much as it was a form of human experience itself." (20)

Perhaps the finest example of this occurred not in one of Olson's readings of his own poetry, but in a reading he gave 10 years later in Buffalo. In this "Gratwick Highlands" talk of that time, Olson called Whitman's "Crossing Brooklyn Ferry," the greatest sermon-poem ever written. Olson recognized, as his class did when he read it in its entirety to them at Buffalo, that Whitman had expressed a primordial reality, had created in his telling of his crossing, a vehicle of re-enactment and a place of presence:

It avails not, time nor place—distance avails not,
I am with you, you men and women of a generation,
  or ever so many generations hence,
Just as you feel when you look on the river and sky,
  so I felt,

Just as any of you is one of a living crowd, I was one
   of a crowd,
Just as you are refresh'd by the gladness of the river and
   the bright flow, I was refresh'd...

Charles Boer, one of Olson's students in Buffalo, relates the story of Olson reading this poem to his class in Buffalo: "It was as if you became Walt Whitman. This was his voice....Olson and Whitman were one. We were all suddenly one." (Boer, 54)

But in 1953 Olson had not reached that point in any of his poems or perhaps in his reading of anyone's poems. In 1953, Olson qualifies that the storyteller, the muthologist, must get the story right. And this leads him, through Thomson again, to the etymology of the term *history*. Thomson explains that the term, *istorin*, as Herodotus first used it, meant "finding out for oneself." (63) This explains why Olson prefers Herodotus to Thucydides. The verbal base of history as method is action: finding out and telling. The act of history, like the rites and practices of Cro-Magnon man that Olson examines earlier in his lectures, is generative and open, not descriptive and closed. It is a form of experience, not a description of experience.

Olson adds one more term to his investigation of word origins to form his generative cluster for these lectures. To 'istorin' and mythos (to find out and to tell), he adds *initiate*. To find out for oneself, in the context of the other sciences he sites, is to go back to origins, to the initial. Doing so initiates the person in an active knowledge of place (geography), past (archaeology and history), and self (mythology and biology, or, the compound he uses once in these lectures physio-psychology). All of which is counter to knowledge as an accumulation of data or collection of information. It is knowing as a verb, knowing embedded in one's presence in space and time, knowing as an uncovering and articulating of self in its spatial and temporal coordinates—and for him as poet, it means that *telling*, as a form of experience, precedes knowing. Olson's belief here is that *doing* precedes knowing, that is, we do before we know what we do.

When listening to the Black Mountain students in Cathryn Zommer's documentary *Fully Awake: Black Mountain College*, Olson's view does not seem personal or idiosyncratic, rather it seems consistent with the educational philosophy at Black Mountain and Olson's participation in the processes of education there. (Albers insistence on understanding color by using it and experiencing it in the eye's response, and not in theory, was undoubtedly one of Olson's pedagogical influences.)

But Olson doesn't stop there in the lectures. He continues to mine Jung and Kerenyi in searching for the active relevance of myth. It is not surprising, given the importance he gives to biology and geography among the sciences, that he brings mythology back to the body and the earth.

Olson underlined in his copy of *Essays on the Science of Mythology*, Jung's statement that "The symbols of the self arise in the depths of the body and they express its materiality" (92). Later in that paragraph, Jung agrees with Kerenyi:

> "at bottom" the psyche is simply "world." In this sense I hold Kerenyi to be absolutely right when he says that in the symbol the *world itself* is speaking. The more archaic and "deeper," that is the more *physiological*, the symbol is, the more collective and universal, the more "material" it is. (92)

Although favorably noting this passage, Olson takes exception to the word *symbol*, particularly when used later by Jung in the phrase "symbol-making." Instead there, Olson prefers the "act of image."

In his lectures, Olson defines *image* as the final form of a metamorphic, physical process. Where Jung appears satisfied with symbol as a visual image, Olson infers that it should, rather, be understood as the result of the *process* of making form, of transforming. Olson finds confirmation of his sense, as poet, of the act of image in Linneaus' definition, as used in entomology, of *imago*: "the final and perfect stage or form of an insect after its metamorphoses; the 'perfect insect'." (74)

Olson fully realizes the import of image to myth much later. Again in *Poetry and Truth*:

> the experience of image or vision is...simply an entrance into our own self...our dogmatic conditions...

which we inherit by being alive and acquire by seeking to be alive. (44)

And importantly, for Olson, the primary source of a person's mythological present, the initial[2] human experience that informs the mythological for a person, is his or her experience of the earth.

Surprisingly then, in *The Chiasma* lectures, Olson spends very little time discussing the earth or geography. He favorably mentions both Carl Sauer and Edgar Anderson, and cites Sauer's studies of the importance of the ice age, how ice shaped and reshaped the earth and mankind's experience of the earth, but he does not expand upon those ideas other than to note how human migration traces human interaction with the earth—noting particularly Anderson's claim that many of the earth's plants are actually artifacts; they would not be and would not be what they are without man's engagement and movement. Anderson writes that man "lives surrounded by transported landscapes, that our commonest everyday plants have been transformed by their long associations with us so that many roadside and dooryard plants are artifacts." (99) Although this passage from Anderson resonates with Olson's statements about the act of image, it says very little about an embodied, particularexperience of

---

2   I use the word initial here in the root sense in which Olson used it ("initia means to begin to find out" (Special View of History 21)). Experience of the earth is initiation into place and space.

the earth and mythology.

Only later in *The Chiasma*, does Olson make the connection. He does so when he draws from the French classicist's, Victor Berard's, work on *The Odyssey*. He notes that Berard shows how Homer used places and place names as the base of his stories. Berard catalogs a number of the names and places in The Odyssey, including a crater filled island and the island that is a "rock like a ship" (Corcyra from the Semitic name Korcyra). In *The Chiasma* lectures, Olson talks about these places and names and how Homer used the cratered island, for instance, and flipped the horizontal to the vertical to create his land of the one-eyed monsters and the figure of the Cyclops.

That is a clear example of myth and the transformative act of image, but it says little about the personal experience of the earth and the telling of that. Once again it isn't until later in this life that Olson more fully discusses this sense of the experience of the earth and mythology. He does so in his 1965 lectures in Vancouver titled *Causal Mythology*. At that later date Olson states clearly what he intimated in 1953:

> I find myself constantly returning to that unit, Earth as orb, as though it was to suggest that if there is any legitimacy to the word that we call mythology it is literally the activeness, the possible activeness and personalness of experiencing it as such. (9)

Active, personal experience of the earth becomes

increasingly pronounced in the late Maximus poems...
but is not the case in the *Maximus* poems Olson wrote
at the time of *The Chiasma* lectures. In fact, it isn't until
those late poems that Olson lets go of the Maximus
persona and seems finally to be speaking directly
from his own mythological present. It is striking
for all his talk of "doing before knowing" that the
lectures and understanding of 1953 required some 12-
15 years of writing, reading, and talking (his *doings*)
for these concepts and definitions of myth to be fully
internalized. In many poems from 1965 on, Olson
actualizes the point he makes in his 1968 lecture
Poetry *and Truth*. There he says:

> today [we] are terribly prone to speak of mythology
> as though it was a social condition, when I'm con-
> vinced mythology has never been anything but...
> [how] one lives one's image (33-34)[3]

---

3   Olson enacts this point in a late Maximus poem (pages 577-
78). I concluded the talk with a reading of this poem in which the
sun speaks to Olson and Olson gives voice to its message.

Works Cited

Boer, Charles. 1975. *Charles Olson in Connecticut* (Swallow Press)

Jung, Carl and Carl Kerenyi. 1969. *Essays on the Science of Mythology* (Princeton University Press)

Olson, Charles. 1969. *Causal Mythology* (San Francisco: Four Seasons Foundation)

1970. *The Special View of History*, ed. Anne Charters (Berkeley: Oyez Press)

1971. *Poetry and Truth: The Beloit Lectures and Poems*, transcribed and edited George Butterick (San Francisco: Four Seasons Foundation) 1978. *The Chiasma, or Lectures in the New Sciences of Man* in *Olson: The Journal of the Charles Olson Archives* (Storrs, CT: no. 10)

Charles Alexander

dear Charles,

"an actual earth of value" is hard to find these days, when we seem so distanced from dirt and water and sky, when so much of our activity is electronic, so many of our friendships are formed without ever touching a hand or sharing a meal. You saw loss all around, and you were right to see it, and also right to see the wonder, i.e. that "earthly paradise" you said you were "going to hate to leave" toward the end of the Maximus poems.

I sought your work out when I was about 20 years old, sought to know those who knew you when I was 24 and first met Bob Creeley & Ed Dorn & Robert Duncan & Anselm Hollo & Nate Mackey. Such meetings have turned into a life. Now it's 37 years later, and I have read just about everything you ever wrote that has been published, and some that is in your archive, and I never tire of it. The work lives in that transference of value, in that complexity of wonder, akin to what Fanny Howe called "bewilderment."

I've heard some people say they like your whole poems that seem to finish, as do I – yes, you had me with Cole's Island and Moonset, Gloucester, but increasingly you have me with the little motes and atomic moments of a phrase running diagonally on a large page in Maximus II or III, possibly with a parenthetical remark, maybe a date, and nothing else on the page, as though our words are moments of recognition amid a landscape, or amid an hour (or minute?) of thought, and such words themselves are mini-polises, places we take some time to walk around and come to understand their value. You tried to give us SPACE, but you also gave us time, you still give me time.

You have opened something for many, for all of us, and I hope I have made a push in that opening as well, in how I utter words into the air and onto paper, in how I consider the art I make as a part of everything. If I do a bit of that, it is always in part in honor of you, sometimes directly because of you.

No matter where/when we are, we are always "afterwards, in between, and since." There with you.

love is the force "is the heart, turning"

love,
Charles

Basil King

Dear Charles:

I find you returning again and again. Some of this was first published in 2003 in Steve Dickison and David Meltzer's magazine *Shuffle Boil*. Other parts appeared in my books *mirage: a poem in 22 sections* (Marsh Hawk, 2003) and *Learning to Draw* (Skylight Press, 2011). I wrote a forward for Kyle Schlesinger's book *Charles Olson at Goddard Collage* in 2011 and heard you in class again. Other parts of this piece have never been published before.

I have no intention of writing a Requiem for you or Black Mountain. Socialism, Communism, Fascism— memory is history. America welcomes most immigrants but there is no melting pot. Everyone is reminded, even the Brahmans of Boston, that they came over, and even the American Indian is judged and expected to prove that there is an "American Dream."

Get rich. Be rich. Get rich. Be rich.

And what of Olson? You worked for Franklin Roosevelt. You left the government and went back to your neighbors, their houses, their tables, children, your Irish mother. You changed your devotions. You went and hunted "among stones." And with stones you built a foundation the root of which thrives. The artist knows that you find, you do not search for change.

Politicians vote in laws after the change has already taken place. The redundancy haunts us. Incompleted ideas like chips from a planed piece of wood lie dormant on the floor.

Drink the poet's vernacular
Eat the painter's roughage
Lilies Marigolds Pansies
Apples and Cabbages
Draw me I come to you
When you least expect

Black Mountain College was founded on hope and exhilaration permeates its memory.

Serial
Music
Continues

You arrived at Black Mountain College
Fertile mind
Graceful hands
Cigarettes galore
Long legs
A deck of cards
Language
Language
Language
Eros seeds
Mercury eats in the dining hall

Jung is in the library
Dante drives the truck
Jack builds the Pot Shop
Homer
Pound
Merce of Egypt
The lake
Gloucester
Baseball
Ahab
Melville sits in the Quiet House
The kitchen
Late night coffee
History

Olson, Connie, and baby Kate were sitting on the grass. I had been told that Olson was a big man. The Olson's were back from Yucatan surrounded by an enthusiastic group asking questions. I was introduced. And then he stood up. Six foot-seven inches or was it eight? I'd known a man that size. Basil Henriques was six foot-seven. My father was five-foot-one and when he met the later to be Sir Basil at the Fabian Society Henriques sought him out. "I'm told you read and write Yiddish, modern and old Hebrew, will you teach me?" And when Henriques (called the Gaffer) and his wife Rose built Basil House, the settlement for boys and girls in the East End of London, my father went to work for him.

In 1951 the kitchen was always open and at night

there was coffee. On one of the nights Charles came in. "What are you reading, Boy?" I handed him a 12-page typed letter from my father with underlinings in red. He read it slowly, gave it back and said, "It never changes."

The Black Mountain that I knew was Charles' Black Mountain and he used it as a wedge to create Maximus. It was so long ago but I still remember a person could get caught in the Olson current. He had power.

I brought a poem to class. "Alpha Road" was about events that took place after a V2 dropped in the field at the end of our road. Charles banged his fist on the table and said I didn't live on Alpha Road. "But I did. We lived in 89 and my uncle Lew and aunt Jenny and my cousin Renee lived in 91. Johnny Haynes and his mother lived in 92." Charles was furious. He did not want me to have Alpha.

Charles was the master and I was not always the willing student. I went away and came back several times. I didn't want another father. I already had one. But he was like a father when after my car accident he told me I must not go to jail. When Black Mountain was closing he told me not to go back to New York. Mirage, mirage, I've seen mirages in the desert and on a road while waiting for a ride. This and much more is in my long poem *mirage*.

New students would arrive and before you had a chance to say hello they were gone. You had to be ambitious if you were going to stay at Black Mountain.

The last time I came back the kitchen and dining

hall were closed. The cooks were gone and everyone was cooking for themselves. I had no money so I devised a plan. I would cook and eat supper with everyone who gave me $2. I didn't cook on Sunday and we ate leftovers. Four people signed up and then there were six. Twelve to fourteen dollars bought a lot of food in the 1950s.

I had been by myself for two days. It was Easter break and I had no money. I stayed in the studio working. You came looking for me. You thought maybe I had left. You knew I was lonely and having a hard time with my work. You looked at all the paintings I had done. They were oils on paper and they were on the walls and on the floor. You said: WOW! This should give you a lift. We went up to your house and you brought out a Pinch Bottle, good Scotch, and Betty made food and it was friendly. You told me you were very concerned that so many of the students were veterans who had gone into the army right after high school and you didn't know what they were going to do when they left the protection of Black Mountain. We talked about the possibility of another war and I said my generation of Europeans would never go to war. You didn't say anything. I remember we finished the bottle.

1983: I wanted to draw Charles. I wrote George Butterick at the University of Connecticut. We had never met. He said that he had photographs and I should come up and choose which ones I wanted. At the library George showed me a letter that I had written

to Charles after Martha and I moved in together. It was
a letter that a son writes a father. I told him that I was
in love.

> Olson had found Maximus
> and brought him
> to Black Mountain.
> He brought him
> in his father's mail bag.
> He brought him from New England
> so Melville
> so Whale so Raven
> did Poe when he
> was in New York
> so Charles
> wrote across
>
> the blackboard
> with white hands
> and white chalk
>
> you drew
> for us
> the distance
> and that was
> to learn division.

The Forbidden Planet is a 1956 science fiction
film directed by Fred M. Wilcox and starring Walter
Pidgeon, Anne Francis and Leslie Nielsen. The plot,

characters and setting all inspired by Shakespeare's *Tempest*. It played in the movie theater in Black Mountain and some of us went back two or more times. I can still see Charles wiggling in his seat he loved it so. I remember the electronic music by Louis and Bebe Barron was exceptional.

What isn't in my poem *mirage* or any other piece that I've written is why I came back the last time. I had decided to graduate. I was putting a graduation program together with Wes and Charles. Charles came into my studio and said he was going to announce that night the school was closing.

Oh, Black Mountain wonderful place
Desperate place.
I was blown to where light abstracts the smallest thing
Into the core of a vernacular
Into the heart of the abstract
No wind but the stillness blows me, no reason
No existence blows the shapes that have lost their edges
Oh, Black Mountain wonderful place
Desperate place
Blow your feathers and your worms
Your mulch protrudes the surface
Your bravery blows forgiveness
Your anger blows freedom

Oh, Black Mountain wonderful place
Desperate place

I was blown to where light abstracts the smallest thing
Into the core of a vernacular
Into the heart of the abstract
No wind but the stillness blows me, no reason
No existence blows the shapes that have lost their edges.

###

Ruth Lepson

Snow and Dry Stones

George Quasha, my poetry teacher at SUNY Stony Brook, knew all about and knew the Black Mountain poets, as did Eliot Weinberger, whom George talked into transferring from Yale to Stony Brook, where the poetry was happening, in 1967. They were my first mentors.

George brought Denise Levertov, Robert Creeley, Robert Duncan to campus and sometimes I imagine he brought Olson too but that's a hallucination stemming from a wish.

The Objectivists, whom Eliot was keen on, and the Black Mountain poets were the suggested reading then, in the midst of a drug haze and an endless stream of musicians coming to campus, thanks to *Crawdaddy* magazine's editors on campus, who wrote the first philosophical essays about rock bands.

And George rented a bus to take us all to hear Louis Zukofsky at the Guggenheim and we sat enraptured despite the softness of his voice, as he was old and frail by then.

For me Creeley became instantly the most essential poet, with Denise a close second, and over the years I heard her maybe 12 or 15 times. Creeley became a friend and still I visit him at Mt. Auburn Cemetery in Cambridge, just a short walk from my house. I ask him how he feels about the English landscape that surrounds him—he doesn't seem to mind.

I read Olson but he wasn't on my radar again until I moved to Boston in the 70's. Sometimes I would go to Gloucester, stay at the Ocean View Inn, sit at Bass Rocks and sketch or grade papers or just climb the rocks or walk along Atlantic Ave.

There was an Olson conference, must have been 2005—George was there, and Creeley—and afterwards a party at Gerrit Lansing's house, Gerrit having been very close to Olson when Gerrit lived at Hammond Castle on the coast and later in various apartments and his own home. Gerrit tells me Olson didn't cook so Gerrit would make dinner and they were off and running.

Through Gerrit I got to know Olson's Gloucester better—his apartment, the places he wrote about in *Maximus*, the people he knew who were still living there. A rough and tumble world, as John Giglio, who lives on Gerrit's third floor, can attest—he grew up there & told us stories about violence on the docks and friends who died of drug overdoses. Later John lived in Olson's place with Linda, Olson's assistant, after Olson's death.

Without Olson Gloucester would have meant little to poets but now with Vincent Ferrini's old studio turned skillfully and devotedly by his nephew Henry into The Gloucester Writers Center, and Gerrit knowing him and being such a force in his own right, and younger innovative poets like Jim Dunn, Amanda and James Cook, Patrick Doud, Frank Rich in the area, it remains a draw, a big draw.

Two years ago it was my turn to rent a bus—to take my students and a few students from Jill Gatlin's class on an actual field trip to Gloucester. They ran around like mountain goats, so excited to be out of their practice rooms at the New England Conservatory. James Cook talked to us at the Writers Center about the town and Olson, and we saw Olson's apartment, walked around Main Street, ran over to Half Moon Beach and to Hammond Castle, where they jumped over fences to get to the ocean and to neighboring houses—Olson would have approved. This after watching Henry Ferrini's magnificent film *Polis Is This*, which made them clamber to get to the actual town.

What does Olson mean to me? More, as a woman, then I ever thought he would. Diane di Prima, who was the featured reader at an Olson conference, when I asked her whether she thought his work was quintessentially male, said no. Look at the myths and his relation to the Earth, she said.

Having read and reread Creeley on Olson, Levertov on Olson, Duncan on Olson, critics on Olson, and lately having paid attention to Larry Eigner, I know that projective verse, or organic verse as Denise calls it, or poetry by field—which overlap—is the poetry of our time that will survive, and which is essentially multicultural because, in part, as Creeley said, he learned to write poetry from listening to Charlie Parker on Boylston St. in Boston instead of going to his classes at Harvard, while Olson found the Maya, Melville, and the fisherman's life.

Now I'm reading Nathaniel Mackey, and as T. J. Anderson points out in his really astute essay on Mackey, Olson incorporated larger structures and many more parts of the Earth and in history than poetry in the U.S. had previously.

*

The snow from the last storm had covered the branches of the maples. Today's storm is filling the spaces between the porch and the sidewalk so there's no room to walk. I think of Olson in Henry Ferrini's film *Polis Is This* walking in the harsh and beautiful winter in Gloucester and of the times he worked as a postman, noticing the particulars of weather, houses, people and animals along his route. Energy, the local, the swirling of molecules of all kinds in this human and other universe.

I think of the day in high school when my English teacher read Hopkins and Eliot to us and having never heard such things or known one could put into words such things I went home and wrote my own silly poem about two roses: one, an artificial rose in vase in a house, the other a wild rose, living among the elements and experiencing the world. I was trying to get at something I would find some years later, reading the poetry of Creeley, Levertov, Olson, Duncan, Zukofsky, Oppen, Bronk, and others who would claim the essential places in the making of a new world of poetry.

That's a grand claim but, after Stein and Williams and Pound, they gave us what we needed to continue, for language to be living again. Having left music to write poetry, I was unsure where life would take me but when I got to Stony Brook and read and heard these poets I was ready to commit myself to poetry or rather it took hold of me as something filled with the combustible energies of the living, something new, flexible, specific, bodily, that came from the freedom to pay attention, to read widely, to find another way that went below the radar of the commercial, loud-mouthed, manipulative capitalist Western world. Even a way to protest the horrors of war— or not protest so much as find an alternative.

Well, the torture of the Earth and our fellow creatures continues, what Olson had warned us against.

He hated the construction of Route 128, which allows us in Boston to get to Gloucester so easily. He hated the tearing down of old houses and wrote editorials railing against that. He knew the history of Gloucester perhaps more deeply than anyone else had, because he saw the layers of history, geography, and family life it held. He kept walking, among the ruins.

What must it have been like to have that kind of energy, to teach all night and all the next day, never to tire of talking and walking and smoking and drinking. (And Olson never tired of teaching.) I think of Larry

Eigner, his great student. What could proprioception mean to someone without that energy, someone who couldn't walk or get about at all on his own, someone who could type with thumb and forefinger only, watching to world from his porch in Swampscott, as the years swirled around him like today's snow. As it turns out, proprioception is anyone's life, attentively lived, breathed, felt, the sincerity of living in one's senses and rooting oneself in what one experiences, translating that through the breath and the heartbeat and the intellect and of course—what else could it be—an individual way.

The snow is coming down more thickly now and the world out the window looks grey, brown, dark green and white, that rugged beauty. What do we all have in common in the East Coast of America—the trees, sky, houses, weather. Aptly enough, the mailman just put the mail through the slot in the door and what has arrived—through wind and snow, the mailman's head covered in navy blue wool—Simon Pettet's new book, *As a Bee*, which I open to page 30:

POEM (The Necessities)

two oranges
incense
a little water-fire
some tastefully-wilted flowers
a perpetual shining bowl
two cups

The way Olson implies relationships, connections, derivations, the everyday, surely all that has filtered down to the lives of poets such as Simon, a British boy who made himself an American, who dedicated his life to poetry at the expense of life's comforts, who found a community of the likeminded.

And what else has come in the mail, as they say? My W-2 form, Blue Cross bill, bank statement. Olson rather than excluding such matters from the life of the poem took them into consideration, in the ways in which our lives are mitigated by, ruled by, constrained by, altered by those aspects of our material, conforming, time-consuming ways.

Creeley's fragments are the epic of the individual... Olson thought his own epic larger than Pound's or Williams', even. Whether or not that is the case, he has in common with Whitman what Giles Deleuze describes in his essay "Whitman":

> If the fragment is innately American, it is because America itself is made up of federated states and various immigrant peoples (minorities)—everywhere a collection of fragments....The experience of the American writer is inseparable from the American experience....This is what gives the fragmentary work the immediate value of a collective statement.

The world as a collection of heterogeneous

parts: an infinite patchwork, or an endless wall of dry stones (a cemented wall, or the pieces of a puzzle, would reconstitute a totality). The world as a sampling....Selecting singular cases and minor scenes is more important than any consideration of the whole. It is in the fragments that the hidden background appears, be it celestial or demonic.... the fragments must ... be extracted by means of a special act, an act that consists, precisely, in writing....Democracy and Art themselves form a whole only in their relationship with Nature (the open air, light, colors, sounds, the night...); lacking these, art collapses into morbidity, and democracy, into deception....

...the reality of American literature, under these two aspects: spontaneity or the innate feeling for the fragmentary, and the reflection on living relations that must constantly be acquired and created. Spontaneous fragments constitute the element through which, or in the intervals of which, we attain the great and carefully considered visions and sounds of both Nature and History.

from Deleuze's "Bartleby; or, the Formula":

...what Melville [Olson's master] had already said about the American literature of his time: because there are so few authors in America, and because its people are so indifferent, the writer is not in a position to succeed as a recognized master. Even in his failure, the writer remains all the more the bearer of a collective enunciation, which no longer forms part of literary history and preserves the rights of a people to come, or of a human becoming.

T. J. Anderson, in that essay on Nathaniel Mackey, "Interstellar Space," talks about Olson's influence on Mackey (though Duncan was the greater influence):

> Using breath to dictate line placement has musical resonance reflecting the manner in which a musician can modulate a particular tone by controlling his or her breath. This idea returns poetry back to its original, ancient impulse....What Olson brings to poetry is its original impulse to as an oral performance in which sound is not ancillary to meaning. Olson's use of blank space becomes an important element in Mackey's work in which music and the visual aspect of word placement plays a prominent role.

Both poets of the imagination, archaeologists of the morning and of places and spaces far from our time yet buried not too deeply in the earth if one searches.

In a remarkable insight that unifies the lyric to the postmodern, Mackey, in an interview with Ed Foster that Anderson quotes, says "The way in which the heterodox lyric tradition in the West has tried to avail itself of those things that go counter to and are contrary to that very rationalist Cartesian order is one of the things that make the question of the lyric and of subjectivity not as cut and dried as some of the dismissals of the lyric and of subjectivity have tended to suggest."

Jazz, Creeley, Olson, Williams, Pound, and big daddy Whitman. The women—well, there's another matter....

*

A few days later....Willie Loco Alexander of Gloucester sent his beautifully simple and totally fun CD of 2009, which includes poems about sea gulls and sky, as well as his rock version of Olson's letter 27, so the beat goes on.

And two summers ago I had a week in residence at Windhover, an arts center in Rockport, just down the road from Gloucester, with Ammiel Alcalay, Kate Tarlow Morgan, and others who have written about, created artworks in relation to Olson.

With reverence,
Ruth

Tyrone Williams

To the future Master Charlie Rebel,

among the *topos* of our Lord, 1630

Now, reduced to here, this island, discrete, I myself am only I, a thwarted man. Petition after petition to go abroad, to return to the new world I christened New England (I dream, of course, of that day when it will be necessary to rename this spit of land New Britain) for our King (yes, yours too, that pinnacle of divine right you keep trying to flatten into your, as our, manifest destiny), rejected, denied. So I write, for what else can a desailed man do? Yes, I am reduced to a man of letters, the humiliation of the desk and sitting-room. I presume you will have known, and doubtless will have despised, Tennyson's "Ulysses," that house-weary paean to our all-too-soon waning empire (an ache I feel even though I stand on the other side of the bell curve, in ascension). I get it, and though you sit—no, stand— awashed in the glorious light of broken and conflated humors, not unlike your presumptuous United States of America, the genetic flaw, your mortal coil upon itself, has become, shall we posit, rather visible. I know something about this, am told, have heard, they claim, am too familiar.

And so, I am family, one of your ancestors, if not a relative. I remain flattered to be claimed as one of your heroes. You understand, then, the necessity of conquest, the annexation of spatiality by space, one manifold of departure and destination as here we stand. Yes, I too have toppled the tyranny of metaphor, imprisoned it in the cells of my poems. However, I am disturbed by reports from the future prior to yours, this Riemann and his influence on, if not over, you. Yes, I managed to map important sections of the land I dubbed New England. But this mapping, however technical, could not be abstracted into the mathematical idealisms that you derived from Riemannian geometry. This is hardly a defense of Euclid, that other genius of idealism. The earth is neither round nor flat; nor is it a sphere even if it approaches the spherical. You cast out the chimera of metaphor only to sneak it back in under the cover of metonym, a maximum contiguity cobbled together as a metaphysics of materialism. There is, in your various essays on "the getting rid" of this and that, a letting-in that comes or stands between the typewriter and thing, that is, an invited company of things that stand between one thing and another thing. Perhaps this is all due to this thing you dub "literature," which you scorn as that which interferes with what is before us, what can be apprehended by the musket, by the force of speech, though I have found, in my limited experience, nothing gets through the muck like a good sound thrashing...

By then you will have heard the rumors, the alleged mutiny, insurrection, and totalitarianism which I will not deny to you, my brother to come. I confess to these acts but not to their criminalization. For I crossed the sea with a ship of fools, a stiff-necked horde dressed up as "crew" and "passengers." Were it not for me you and your States would not exist. I apologize for nothing, I do not regret, do not look back, put one foot in front of another as I march into the annals which will have chronicled my journeys. You understand a man like me, a man who gets things done, the petty mores and customs of little minds notwithstanding. We are never not at war, and yet my expeditions which demanded the sacrifice of men are used to punish me as though I am to be held accountable for losses without compensations for the gains. I am held up as an "example," penned within the stockade of a people whose very survival remained perilous but for my interventions. What is at issue is neither the events nor their sequence but only the question of interpretation, how these markers are to be held—or if you will, published—as history. I won, triumphed over adversity, raised my savage countrymen to the highest pitch of possibility, and yet, though I put down this history, this mapping, in my own books, they have been overwritten by the envious and poisonous pens of my enemies. I trust you will provide the remedy for these injustices, these bloated travesties, the likes of which are truly unparalleled in the history of our—pardon me, my—great land.

I am once again asea, but this time I have no deck below me, no men around me. I spend my days writing letters to Her Majesty, letters that, I know, go unread, or if read, are scorned, tossed aside as I have been discarded, decommissioned. Usurped by scribblers who write of the savages with no direct knowledge of their habits and customs, who guess at the circumference of seas, rivers, lakes by sight alone, I am bereft, my attention to the particulars of coastal erosion, tidal eddies, reduced to pedantry. You too will suffer this fate, your incompetence at chair-sitting and bluster exposed in all its nakedness, what will be your Big Horn. Call it Black Rock.

Your humble brother,
Captain John Smith

Dale Smith

WHAT YOU ARE /
HOW YOU ARE /
WHERE YOU ARE

through *Maximus*

Blues People, like *The Shoshoneans*,
right out of Olson. The projective experiment—
series of self
disclosures via environment,
an ecstasis of thought, emotion
even just as on a normal day
the laundry and kitchen
the hours of quiet activity
begin far away

*

                Drove north to Mansfield, ON,
with
my kids and close friend
Little snowy cornfields
blanched to whiteness and grey
barns, ancient homes
vast suburban tracts

to endure whiteness

in Ontario intersects my dreaming
of the Loa, a
rhythm of Iwa
          Ezili Dantor
across Atlantic
                    color is the evidence of truth

          The sea far away
reacts as memory, a vast
caramel or turquois of light
against wide tracks
of groundhog or porcupine
along the snow trail.

Olson opened
toward a white blackness—
                white interior
darkened in slurry admixtures
an impossible imposition of
culture on race, the genetic
      slave and master
indebted, crammed

Daydream into the trail
bright day white field
"Family Day"
offering whiskey
to numb cold nose, icy bard beards
little red sumac flowers crunchy
and blood dark, held to twiggy

grey branches   the sky
mottled by thin overcoats
of cloud and pink light
lighting blue fields

Two Americas
black and white

the excursion proved pleasant
children skied
the seasons of corn and harvest,
waste and awakening
cold warmth, commonweal

a larger mythos one might seek
caves under pleasures, reductive
games, a predatory advance unacknowledged
even as sorrow   transparent
advantageous gateways

        shall the gods reign yonder
lost in shadows of proposal?
Iwa
        Ezili Dantor
well

        right here a public noise
on the way for pizza, "there was a Dance Hall there"

at Kent Circle

at Kunt Circle
where Cunt Circle

Dear Feral Maximus
what I seek to stand
against the professions

                    a sexualized geography
of enclosure, careful order

                    the drama

"as quiet as I was
out of the sky as quiet
as the blizzard was"

reaches for signals
            a gnarly narrative
                        dreaming, forgetting

what it means is that to be uncomfortable
with oneself, to arrive uninvited, much too casually
unexplained, awkwardly reaching out over polite table
company   like sitting with important folks
blanking out on conversation   blacking out

because the snow last Monday
or the Niagara-freezing cold
                    the prayed-for glimpse of tiny trilliums

blacking out whiteness Olson's   sheet-covering   New England
fish monger adventurers   "the country not discovera"

Olson's Smith   and the many Smiths

misnamed continentals

in the late evening winter last light
end of long day
                          making fun
the groundwork
unmanageable

                    a heap, variegated, ongoing
                              cosmos

            (whatever City Hall might say)

                    Dufferin County, its rates

Now give quiet offering
to the Black Lady

Joe Safdie

Letter to Olson

When I was in graduate school in Boulder in the late 70s, I was sharing a house with two other creative writing students whom I miss and with whom I wish I were in touch (their names are Oscar and Randy). At one point while living in this quasi-suburban house, I remember throwing the *I Ching* (I always used the sticks, never the coins) and asking whether I should follow the "Olson philosophy" in my poetic life. I probably used other words when I was asking the question and wish I could reproduce them here, as one of the deals when consulting the *I Ching* – as I remember it – was getting one's question down to no more than eight words. Still, the answer was entirely positive. In fact, it was more than just "positive," as I still remember it: it must have been insistent. So what was I really asking the oracle? I think it was whether I should follow mainstream poetics or whether I should be a "rebel." Perhaps that question, in all its infinite manifestations, is still an object of concern to people who write poetry today: I couldn't possibly know.

But the fact is that I hadn't even *heard* of Charles Olson until, in my junior year, I transferred to UC Santa Cruz, and had the great good fortune of taking a two-quarter class from Norman O. Brown, the first of which was on Pound's *Cantos* and the second on people who followed him, including Duncan and Olson. I don't think any of my professors at UCLA, where I spent my first two years, had ever heard of him: it was all Dylan Thomas and Sylvia Plath. Is he on the curriculum for undergraduates now? Probably not. And what does the word "mainstream" even mean these days? In the last 20 years, the AWP has assumed monumental status among creative writers, at least those attached to universities. I ignored them for a long time until I attended one of their annual conferences last year (I had finally published a book of poems and wanted to get other poets to read it). But how many people at this astonishingly huge conference, with hundreds of rows of small press publishers selling their wares, had been similarly influenced by Olson and the Black Mountain aesthetic? The answer, I suspect, is: not many.

Even Nobby (as all his students called him) said – half tongue in cheek – that Olson was a fraud because he didn't really know any Greek. "Let the young / educ the young" is what I remember in this context, and I just looked it up on Google and found it was actually in *Paterson*, a letter from Pound that Williams had reproduced . . . and did Olson then put it in *Maximus*? Dunno. Anyway, that was the lineage for me: Pound and Williams leading to Olson. It's hard to reproduce the excitement of reading things like "Projective Verse" and "Human Universe" for the first time, but it was large. And then, in my second year of graduate school, Ed and Jenny Dorn came to Boulder.

I've written about the experience of being Ed's

student and friend at http://epc.buffalo.edu/authors/dorn/DORN_CENTO/dorn_safdie.html, and even though Ben wanted me to somehow adapt that story as a model for this one, I find that I can't, any more than I can somehow speak to Olson directly in a letter. But I can reproduce sections from another old piece, a review I wrote of two books by Dale Smith and Richard Blevins that wound up talking mostly about Olson. And it turns out that, once formed, those bonds of "legacy" are hard to break: I'm still riding some of the ripples of that tremendous wave, coming back to Eric Havelock to write about the origins of written language, for example, for a textbook I'm writing. I said in a short letter to *House Organ* about the Heriberto Yépez flap that I didn't have the time to devote to that somewhat spurious issue (but I'm glad that Ken Warren and Ammiel Alcalay do, and have used it well). But this is what I did have time for, once upon a time, and still do:

*

from "What I See in Dale Smith's *American Rambler* and Richard Blevins' *Fogbow Bridge*," published in Charles Potts' magazine *The Temple*, Fall 2002

Anyone with more than a passing acquaintance with Charles Olson's work is familiar with the famous beginning of *Call Me Ishmael* – "I take SPACE to be the central fact to man born in America, from Folsom Cave to now." Not as many, however, might know his literary formulation a few paragraphs later – after describing the Great Plains as "the fulcrum of America," he says "Some men ride on such space, others have to fasten themselves like a tent stake to survive. As I see it, Poe dug in and Melville mounted. They are the alternatives."

However accurate this proposition, the writers under review here have adopted the Melvillean alternative, "that travel/travail" as Richard Blevins has it in "Journey to the Source." It's implied in the titles of the books, *American Rambler* and *Fogbow Bridge*, and also, I think, in their methodology. Yet the poems also explore a corresponding stasis, a "rootedness" that can develop as a result of such travel, vertical as opposed to horizontal, inward as opposed to outward. These books, finally, give a sense of how what might be called the "Olson legacy" is being carried and transformed by various practitioners today, after twenty years or so of a quite different poetics being in the ascendant. . . .

I had bought Richard Blevins' *Fogbow Bridge* sometime earlier – largely because I saw Dorn had written a blurb for it and because Blevins had contributed a nice poem to a collection of tributes assembled by Ralph LaCharity, *A Wake for Ed Dorn* – but hadn't read it yet. So, in mid-June, feeling tentatively buoyant at the prospect of my first summer off from teaching in seven years, I started looking through it haphazardly, noting many references to Dorn and Olson and Haniel Long, a central personage in one of the many longer poems collected therein, "Court of the Half-King." At this point, the idea of combining reviews of both books in one essay dawned; I then came across a short poem called "A Good Early Start" which begins

I don't teach again
>   til September
>   and today
>   is June thirteen.

Actually it was the fourteenth, but the coincidence was so sublime that I started making notes immediately! It's through connections like these, after all, that I came to poetry, and it's even possible that the writing I'm drawn to – including, very much, these two books – is *about* the possibility of such connection. Nothing else will (says Olson through Whitehead) do. Or as Dorn has it in *Slinger*, "Everything is prehensible / for from that which is not / we fall off" . . .

I don't think any of us should be talking if any of you haven't taken any one of the hallucinogens, because you really don't know, you're really just talking academically because you ought to have the experience, that's all.
—Charles Olson, "Under the Mushroom"

In addition to the content, the twisted, blunt, stacatto lines and line breaks here [in Smith's *American Rambler*] give a sense of the knotted and tangled nature of the experience, make these lyrics not, as Olson derisively calls lyric in general, "a block in the way of nature," but a passage/wormhole through *to* it; "it's not enough / to imagine it" Smith says, echoing Long's earlier insistence on the necessity of undergoing the experience – "only the whole body / knows what took place." And only through the whole body, one infers, can one attain those healing powers, the capacity to give paradoxically generated by having nothing to give. . . .

How to traverse *is all. . . . This is a transit question: how far does any of us need to go to arrive? . . . We don't know much about transit, why we will go from one place to another.*

Charles Olson, "Under the Mushroom"

So what is the "Olson legacy" anyway? Luckily, there are lots of people still around who knew him and will have, thus, their own particular senses. For me, Olson's admonitions to go *to* it are central: "This is eternity. This now. This foreshortened span." That's from "The Resistance," an early prose piece that was the first one collected in Creeley's *Selected Writings* of 1966 (I own the new, handsome *Collected Prose* but haven't had the heart to start using it), which might have been the first words of his I'd read. That is, no matter how learned or abstruse his references get, his insistence on putting them to *use* – to construct that "actual earth of value" – is what will always stay with me. When I consider the emphasis on (mere) text that's taken hold in the academies and elsewhere these last twenty years, I seem to be in a different world entirely. (In a way, the *project* of both of these books reminds me of the advice Olson had given Dorn in *A Bibliography on America* (1955), that what was important in terms of historical study is "how, as yourself as individual, you are acquiring & using same in acts of form").

Occasionally something he's said will still literally jump off the page. For example, in a panel discussion in Vancouver along with Duncan, Ginsberg, Creeley and Philip Whalen in 1963, he's expounding on his poem "Place; & Name" (a study of which helped immensely in the writing of this review), and he mentions a recent statement by then Secretary of Defense McNamara, to the effect that "nothing is going to happen to us in our lifetime."

> It isn't quite what he said, but as far as I can see it's just exactly a guarantee that really all our worries and fear and the danger has been really organized and set aside, so that there is nothing in our lifetime . . . Like, McNamara does not support *us* in that remarkable projection, right? It just doesn't support us at all. In fact, on the contrary, it accomplishes the end of destruction, which is it destroys us sitting right here. It really just says we're all dreaming right through into some moment later, when this sort of thing will have gone away. It's – what is it? – it's wish-magic, brand new modern wish-magic. Just get rid of it. I think there's a deep split. ("On History," from *Muthologos*, Vol. 1)

No kidding! I leave it to wiser souls to ascertain to what degree this McNamarian vision has become "national missile defense." Later, in "A comprehension," this same "wish-magic" becomes "the new post-European concept of soul as *psyche;* . . . the primary error of analogy as logic instead of image or actualness." The antidote to this poison was always the perception of and attention to minute particulars, "so that gesture and action, born of the earth, may in turn join heaven and hell" ("The Advantage of Literacy") — along with a new/old system of discourse in which "the words and actions reported are set down side by side in the order of their occurrence in nature, instead of by an order of discourse, or 'grammar,' as we have called it, the prior an actual resting on vulgar experience and event." ("Review of Eric Havelock's *Preface to Plato*").

But, you know, either this stuff gets you or it doesn't. It's possible that many practitioners today think Olson is an anachronism, even though there are, happily, others who are mining this rich ground, each in different ways. Enough, perhaps, to conclude with Olson's answer to the question he poses about transit at the beginning of this section, in the talk called "Under the Mushroom": "It's not some step that you take easily, or that even to take the step means anything more than you know without taking the step, if you stop to think about it. You're just who you are; what you do, if it's any good, is true; and you are capable of being alive because of love."

Joshua Corey/Hannah Arendt

Letter to Olson as the Master [unsent]

Dear Mr. Olson,

This is the true story of Maximus the fox. When you wrote

> so few
> have the polis
> in their eye

you discriminated, did you not, among my Greeks. For no human world destined to outlast the short life span of mortals within it will ever be able to survive without men willing to do what Herodotus was the first to undertake consciously—namely, λεγειν τα εοντα, to say what is.

> topos
> typos
> tropos

We conclude that "the burning of all books of geometry" would not be radically effective. The Olympian gods did not claim to have created the world. Everything is immortal except men. Human activities do violence to nature because they disturb what, in the absence of mortals, would be the eternal quiet of being-forever that rests or swings within itself.

the evidence of
what is said

The earth, myth, the I. But on action depends the world. The world by deed, or mouth. A cutting-out expedition. Your Melville: "the poet but embodies in verse those exaltations of sentiment that a nature like Nelson's, the opportunity being given, vitalizes into acts."

istorin, which makes any one's acts a finding out for him or herself, in other words restores the traum: that we act somewhere at least by seizure, that the objective (example Thucydides, or the latest finest tape-recorder, or any form of record on the spot

—live television or what—is a lie

The subject matter of history in these interruptions.

as against what we know and went on, the dreams—

Without a world between men and nature, there would be eternal movement, but no objectivity.

now he's lost touch with the
Old Testament, which had all that
imagery, and all that swell,
that swell and sweltering, of the
possibilities of life in a human being.

Ever since man learned to master it to such an extent that the destruction of all organic life on earth with man-made instruments has become conceivable and technically possible, he has been alienated from nature. Ever since a deeper knowledge of natural processes instilled serious doubts about the existence of natural laws at all, nature itself has assumed a sinister aspect. Deadly danger to any civilization is no longer likely to come from without.

a quality of entanglement or connection to

The social realm, where the life process has established its own public domain, has let loose an unnatural growth, so to speak, of the natural. Against which the private and intimate, on the one hand, and the political (in the narrower sense of the word), on the other, have proved incapable of defending themselves. The realm of "necessity."

almost like an atavism rather than an image

But I wanted to discuss polis, diametrically opposed to the household that your friend Mr. Duncan talks about, the oikos. The polis was distinguished from the household in that it knew only "equals," whereas the household was the center of the strictest inequality. Fishermen & poets, as you say, of the former. And the latter? We have witnessed the expansion of the oikos, the tyranny of necessity, until it includes the entire world. This is the sinister onset of the social, the cannibalistic universe of discourse, against which you offer: letters. Poems. Pointless stories.

> nature
> is an ambulance

Not being a driver, doubting my English, I wondered for a long time over the reversed letters. E C N A L U B M A. Reading right to left does not come naturally. A bridge I couldn't cross. It's a bridge you battled, isn't it, Mr. Olson? A bridge from Gloucester into the America you feared would swallow it. A bridge into, from, for, the common world.

> Islands
> to islands,
> headlands
> and shores

And you advised us not to be fooled by the universalization of the present. Which puts us in communication, if not in line.

But there was this business, of poets, that all my
                              Jews
were in the fish-house

Your Jews, Mr. Olson? I was once accused of having

no feeling for my people. Who, I asked, has feelings for "people" and not persons? Here perhaps we divide. I do not write a letter to "Gloucester," Mr. Olson, but to you.

> You have love, and no object

Reality is not guaranteed primarily by the "common nature" of all men who constitute it, but rather by the fact that, differences of position and the resulting variety of perspectives notwithstanding, everybody is always concerned with the same object.

> the simplest things
last

The point then is not that there is a lack of public admiration for poetry and philosophy in the modern world, but that such admiration does not constitute a space in which things are saved from destruction by time.

> I am making a mappemunde.
> It is to include my being.

Immortality is homeless, like the poet, like the Jew.

> "My name is NO RACE" address
> Buchenwald   new Altamira cave

The hut is no polis. For this trap was our fox's burrow, and if you wanted to visit him where he was at home, you had to step into his trap. "I have become the best of all foxes," he thought.

> The poetics of such a situation
> are yet to be found out

Nobody knows the nature of traps better than one who sits in a trap his whole life long.

Sincerely,
Hannah Arendt

マリア像（訳者撮影）

、The Cantos, 一九六九年）、四二五頁参照。

ターのポルトガル人漁業共同体の守護聖人で、

た。

人の住む地

ge）教会の

ートの像で、

トに縦帆を

船の「下腹

は何によって可能なのかは、判然としない。た

荒波と接する「下腹部」をあらかじめ補強して

Yorio Hirano

What I See in
The Maximus Poems of Charles Olson

I think *The Maximus Poems* of Charles Olson try to rewrite the history of America from its inception, that is, in the 1620s.

The central drama of *The Maximus Poems* lies in opposition between the fishermen who settled in Gloucester in 1624, and the Puritans who settled in Plymouth in 1620. There are two dimensions to this opposition.

(1) The first dimension appears as the opposition between the people of Gloucester and the Plymouth Puritans, struggling over the right for using the "fishing stage of Cape Ann."

"Maximus to Gloucester, Letter 11" shows how dangerous this opposition became. The famous inscription of the Tablet Rock praises the necessary wisdom which stopped the oncoming bloody strife between Gloucester fishermen and Plymouth Puritans. It was in 1625 when their strife nearly demanded bloodshed.

Let us look back and detect the origin of strife over the "fishing stage of Cape Ann." The "fishing stage of Cape Ann" was built by Plymouth Puritans in 1624. However, it was merely built, not used. The people of Plymouth left the "fishing stage" alone. And, in 1625,

Gloucester fishermen used the "fishing stage" for the purpose of FISHING. The people of Plymouth harshly criticized the Gloucester fishermen. This was the root of the strife between them.

The strife heightened and everyone thought the bloodshed was inevitable. However, the bloodshed was avoided by the order of Roger Conant, the first governor of the Massachusetts Bay Colony. The Tablet Rock was built to memorialize the wise arbitration of Roger Conant. The inscription of the Tablet Rock reads:

On this site
in 1623
A company of fishermen and farmers from Dorchester,
Eng. under the direction of Rev. John White founded The
Massachusetts Bay Colony

---

here in 1625 Gov. Roger Conant by wise diplomacy
averted bloodshed between contending factors
one led by Myles Standish of Plymouth
the other by Capt. Hewes
a notable exemplification of arbitration
in the beginning of New England

(Butterick, Guide 77)

The inscription of the Tablet Rock narrates the beginning of Gloucester as the earliest fishing plantation of Dorchester Company, and praises the "wise diplomacy" of Roger Conant.

"Maximus, to Gloucester, Letter 11," first refers to the inscription of the Tablet Rock (line 1 to 3), then describes the battle between Gloucester fishermen and Plymouth Puritans.

> "In the Early History
> A Notable Exemplification of
> Arbitration"
>
> And the Short Chimney
> wld have died right there, been plugged by a fisherman if
> Conant had not ordered Capt Hewes to lower his gun, to
>   listen
> to what the little man from Plymouth had to squawk about
>
> Mister Standish
> wld have been the first to lie in the cemetery where my
>   father does
>
>   (Maximus 52)

Miles Standish, the agent solder of the Plymouth Puritans, is called the
"Short Chimney," because he was short in height and quick-tempered. Standish was nearly shot to death by Captain Hewes, who led Gloucester fishermen.

The voice of the narrator is taunting Miles Standish. Even though he was hot-tempered and short in height, he was a professional soldier. He is depicted as an obdurate and honest soldier in "The Courtship of Miles Standish," written by Henry Wadsworth Longfellow. Here, the narrator makes a fool of Standish. The fact that a professional soldier was nearly shot to death by a fisherman is somewhat strange. However, the strangeness works as a "key" to interpret the situation. The narrator, Maximus, is evidently on the side of the Gloucester fishermen. He does not allow the Plymouth Puritans to criticize his people. Neither does he permit Miles Standish to harm the people of Gloucester. The narrator of the story, Maximus, is heavily biased by his distrust of the Puritans. The narrator's distrust of them is a "key" to unlocking the significance of *The Maximus Poems*.

See again the "wise diplomacy" of Roger Conant, praised in the inscription of the Tablet Rock. The principle of Plymouth people and that of Gloucester people never go together. Two principles cannot but collide. So "arbitration" proves to be very important, as the inscription of the Tablet Rock says.

Roger Conant was born in 1592 and died in 1679, age 88. Conant was **the** governor of Massachusetts Bay Colony from 1623 to 1626. In these three years Dorchester Company sent settlers from England to Cape Ann. In 1626, Conant led a group of settlers to Naumkeag (later called Salem), and finally moved from Salem to Beverly. Conant founded Beverly to live a calm life. However, the people of Salem, the neighboring town of Beverly, called "Beverly" as "Beggarly," the town of beggars. Conant felt very sad over such a contemptuous word. "Letter 10" of *The Maximus Poems* narrates this story.

John Endecott (1584-1665) succeeded Roger Conant and became the Governor of The Massachusetts Bay

Colony. The Dorchester Company advised Endecott to be kind to the Old Planters (that is, Conant's company) and give them equal rights as the New Planters. However, what Endecott did first was to move Conant's house from Cape Ann to Salem.

It is a sign, that first house, Roger Conant's, there, State
                                        Fort. One of
     Endecott's first acts
was to have it dragged to Salem for his own mansion,
                                   for the big house,
the frame of it was that sound, that handsome, the old
                                        carpentry

                    (Maximus 49)

Roger Conant was betrayed by his successor John Endecott. The chain of betrayal did not stop in Endecott. Roger Conant was betrayed by his descendant, James Bryant Conant, who was born in 1893. James Bryant Conant was the president of Harvard University from 1933 to 1953. He asked the State of Oregon to send the best student to Harvard. He abandoned the "localism" of Harvard, and "destroyed" the university.

"Letter 10" reads:

          Harvard
owns too much

          and so its President
          after destroying its localism ("meatballs",
          they called the city fellers, the public school

graduates) Conant destroyed Harvard
by asking Oregon
to send its brightest.

Roger Conant did not destroy, was, in fact, himself
destroyed, as was the city, 1626

(Maximus 51)

James Bryant Conant is criticized by Maximus as a "destroyer of Harvard." In contrast to J. B. Conant, our Roger Conant was not a destroyer, but a man who was destroyed as well as Beverly, the town he had founded.

The greatness of Roger Conant was not succeeded by his successor, John Endecott, nor to his descendant James Bryant Conant. The greatness of Roger Conant was reduced to nothing by the people who sought personal profits. Maximus shows such a history of deterioration to us, that is, what was good in the beginning becomes bad from generation to generation. The result is horrible. Endecott robbed Roger Conant of everything. "Letter 10" reads:

he [Conant] who left his Tudor house, left fishing,
and lost everything to Endecott, lost the colony
to the first of,
        shrinkers

(Maximus 50)

In the beginning of this talk, I suggested that

the central drama of *The Maximus Poems* lies in the opposition between the fishermen who settled in Gloucester in 1624, and the Puritans who settled in Plymouth in 1620. I also suggested that there are two dimensions to this opposition. I think I have talked enough about the first dimension of the opposition. Let us go forward to the second dimension of the opposition.

It is in "Letter 23" we witness again the opposition between the people of Gloucester and the Plymouth Puritans. The opening of "Letter 23" reads:

Letter 23
>   The facts are:
>>   1st season 1623/4 one ship,
>>   the Fellowship   35 tons
>>   with Edward Cribbe as master(? –cf.
>>   below, 3rd season)
>   left 14 men Cape Ann:
>>   John Tilly to oversee the fishing,
>>   Thomas Garner the "planting"[...]
>>   The two of them
>>   "bosses", for a year

But here is the first surprise: all the evidence is, that the Plymouth people, aboard the Charitie [...] got in from England before the above Dorchester fishermen made it, and the Pilgrims had their stage up when these others did arrive, five weeks out of Weymouth. It was this fishing stage which was fought over the next
>   season, when the
Plymouth men returned to find that Westcountry fishermen had preempted it; and Miles Standish was sent for, to fight about it.

(Maximus 103-04)

In the beginning of "Letter 23," we find an explanation of the "STAGE FIGHT." The second dimension of the opposition between Gloucester fishermen and Plymouth Puritans is revealed here.

The first nine lines are the brief explanation for the settlement of Cape Ann. We see again the year-by-year progression of settlement, in "The Picture." (Maximus 119-20)

THE PICTURE

1623 voyage of discovery, ship unknown, Bushrod backer
      (John Watts factor?)
1624   1st season Dorchester Company, *the Fellowship*,
      35 tons, 14 men left Stage Head
1625   2nd season 32 men left, two ships *the Fellowship*
      And the Pilgrimage, 140 tons (which returned
      to England with little more than a third part of her
      lading)

(Maximus 120)

However, it is clear that the first nine lines of "Letter 23" are a much more detailed description of the 1st season of settlement than that of "THE PICTURE." Who directed the fishing, and who guided the agriculture, are written in "Letter 23." We have already read lines 6 and 7:

John Tilly to oversee the fishing,
Thomas Garner the "planting"

(Maximus 120)

140

We find that the dignified statement of history is developed around these lines.

In the passage following these lines, we see that the design of Dorchester Company, that is, building a fishing plantation in the New World, is being realized one by one. We watch the outcome of the grand design with breathless interest, because Maximus tells us the true founding history of America, instead of the false founding history of America, represented by Plymouth Puritans.

However, the re-writing of **the** founding history of America does not go smoothly. The right of using the "fishing stage" prevents the Dorchester Company from realizing their grand design and consequently blocks the re-writing of **the** founding history of America.

See the passage following line 10 of "Letter 23." Line 10 reads: "But here is the first surprise." The "first surprise" is the fact that the Puritans had come to Cape Ann earlier than the Gloucester fishermen, and that the Plymouth Puritans had already built the fishing stage before the Gloucester fishermen. The fishermen and farmers whom the Dorchester Company sent to establish the fishing plantation at Cape Ann were preceded by the Puritans whose aims were establishment of the state which enables oneness of religion and politics. What an irony of history do we see here!

The passage beginning with the "Pilgrims had

their stage up" in "Letter 23" shows the situation in detail. It is natural that the Plymouth Puritans got angry when they knew their fishing stage was used by the Dorchester fishermen without permission. The Puritans sent for Miles Standish to take back the fishing stage from the Gloucester fishermen.

However, it is doubtful why the fishing stage of Cape Ann was necessary for the Plymouth Puritans. The fishing stage of Cape Ann was too far for the Plymouth Puritans to use. The fishing stage does not seem necessary for the Plymouth Puritans.

According to the Rev. William Hubbard's *General History of New England* (1815), the fishing stage of Cape Ann was necessary for the Plymouth Puritans. The Plymouth Puritans had obtained the useless patent for settling Cape Ann, from King James I of England. To make this patent useful they sent a few ships to England in 1623. They expected that the merchant adventures in England would call for the passengers to America. The aim of the passengers was fishing trade in the New World. It was for this purpose that Plymouth Puritans made their fishing stage at Cape Ann in 1624. (Butterick, *A Guide* 167)

The fishing stage was no nonsense either for **the** Gloucester people or for the Plymouth Puritans. Both sides claimed their own rights, and never conceded. Then, came the crisis. Here we can see one of the textual characteristics of *The Maximus Poems*. The beginning of "Letter 23" explains "Letter 11." In reading *The Maximus Poems* we sometimes come across a poem or passage which explains the preceding poem or passage. Olson is a scholar poet. He writes, and examines, and writes again. So an event is written, re-written, and revised in *The Maximus Poems*. The fight over the fishing state is re-written in "History is the Memory of Time."

History is the Memory of Time

That year the STAGE FIGHT [1625/1626]—and as much a Western as
why not, with Hewes' men backed up on the stage they'd taken
by right of hand from Plymouth poor Johns hadn't yet got to
fishing that season (stayed in bed)
                                    Miles Standish,
probably looking just like they tell us coal shuttle,
on head silly pistol cocked at Hewes' chest slashed trousers
ballooning over bow legs
                                    (Maximus 116)

This is the third time we read about the "STAGE FIGHT." The year of the "FIGHT" is corrected from "1625" (inscription of the Tablet Rock) to "1625/1626." *The Maximus Poems* proceeds in this way.

What is narrated is almost identical. However, the narrator's contempt **of** the Plymouth Puritans has become stronger than in the earlier version of the STAGE FIGHT. The Plymouth people are referred to as "Plymouth poor Johns." The Plymouth people are regarded as "dried cods," that is, weaklings. Compared with the Gloucester fishermen, the narrator Maximus says, the Plymouth Puritans are just "dried cods," which don't go fishing and stay in bed.

Captain Miles Standish, who took sides with the Plymouth Puritans, is fully caricatured. The man who seemed to hold "coal shuttle" on his head, called "Short Chimney" ("*Letter 11*"), had his "slashed trousers/ ballooning over his bow legs." This description reminds us of a gun-fight scene in a Western, or in comic strips. However, what is important is not the difference between the opening of "*Letter 23*" and "*History is the Memory of Time.*" What is important is the fact that the identical event is depicted again and again with a slight difference.

There are decisively important moments of history in *The Maximus Poems*, to which Maximus returns several times. One such moment is the opposition between the Plymouth Puritans and the Gloucester fishermen. It is a moment when the Puritan ideals of founding America clashed with the daily lives of naïve Gloucester fishermen who settled in Cape Ann. This is the moment when the two founding histories clashed with each other. Puritans sought the union of religion and politics in the New World. The aim of the Dorchester Company and the Gloucester fishermen was fishing. This is the second dimension of the opposition.

The latter half of "*Letter 23*" reads:

What we have here—and literally in my own front yard, as I sd to Merk, asking him what delving,

into "fishermans ffield" recent historians...   not telling
him it was a poem I was interested in, aware I'd scare
him off, [...]

I would be a historian as Herodotus as, looking
for oneself for the evidence of
what is said [...]

What we have in this field in these scraps among these fishermen,
and the Plymouth men, is more than the fight of one colony with
another, it is the whole engagement against (1) mercantilism [...
                              and (2) against
nascent capitalism except as it stays the individual adventurer
and the worker on shore—against all sliding statism, ownership
getting in to, the community as, Chamber of Commerce, or theocracy;
or City Manager

(Maximus 104-05)

The first passage narrates that the strife between
the Gloucester people and the Plymouth Puritans
occurred "literally in my own front yard." The
simple phrase "my own front yard" contains a
problem. Olson himself enters into the text and
takes over the position of the narrator Maximus
without any explanation. Readers of *The Maximus
Poems* often experience this kind of violation and
they are accustomed to this kind of non-modernist
text in which the author and the narrator are
easily switched. "[M]y own front yard" is the front
yard of the summer house where Olson spent summer
with his parents when he was a boy. We do not know
whether the author Olson plays the part of the narrator
Maximus, or the narrator Maximus contains the author
Olson in himself.

"Merk" in line 1, who is treated as a friend of the narrator, is Frederick Merk, a historian at Harvard University. When Olson was a student at Harvard, he took Frederick Merk's course, "Westward Movement," and was much influenced. However, in lines 1 through 4, Olson makes himself appear more learned than his former teacher.

There are two reasons why Olson behaves like this. Reason number 1: The "STAGE FIGHT" took place in his own front yard. Olson knows the place where "STAGE FIGHT" occurred since he was a child. His knowledge was not the bookish one, but the lived one. Reason number 2: Aristotle wrote in his *Poetics* that the poet is superior to the historian because the poet can write what probably happens, whereas the historian can write just what happened in the past. These two reasons explain why Olson takes a superior attitude to Frederick Merk.

The second passage reads: "I would be a historian as Herodotus was." Olson declares here that he will follow the method of Herodotus when he writes *The Maximus Poems*. The method was "looking for the evidence of what is said."

The third passage narrates the "STAGE FIGHT" again, but the perspective is different from the description of the "STAGE FIGHT" preceding this passage. The opposition between the Gloucester fishermen and the Plymouth Puritans is not just the strife over the "fishing stage." There is an absolute difference between the Gloucester peoples' way of living by fishing, and the Plymouth Puritans' way of living. The latter acquires "(1) mercantilism, and then (2) nascent capitalism."

Olson sees this opposition through the "STAGE FIGHT." The simple and naïve living of the Gloucester people does not go with the Plymouth Puritans' "mercantilism and its nascent capitalism." Olson is a witness to this opposition which has been taking place in his "own front yard" since he was a child. "Letter 16" shows an insight which sees through the corruption of capitalism.

He [Bowditch] represents, then, that movement of NE monies
away from primary production & trade
to the several cankers of profit-making
which have […] made America great.

Meantime, of course, swallowing up
The land and labor.   And now,
   the world.

(Maximus 76)

"NE monies" in line 1 means "New England monies." Nathaniel Bowditch, a member of the administration board at Harvard, is the symbol of "NE monies." He was said to drive out the President John Thornton Kirkland from Harvard, and he made enemies. On the other hand, he was praised because he saved Harvard from financial difficulties.

With his exceptional ability for calculating profits and losses, Bowditch founded several insurance companies. When he was taking charge of cargoes in Salem, he saw to it that the merchant adventurers might make profits. Indeed, Nathaniel Bowditch is a personification of New England money. The first four lines cited above show that New England money represents the power of capitalism itself. It swallows up "the land and labor. And now,/the world."

The evil of capitalism has been corrupting America. A few lines of "Capt Christopher Levett (of York)" presents an idea that the coming of Puritans from England to America "dirtied" the "newness" of the New World.

> one's forced,
> considering America,
> to a single truth: the newness
>
> the first men knew was almost
> from the start dirtied
> by second comers.

(Maximus 138-39)

The "first men" in line 4 are the Dorchester fishermen. And the "second comers" in the final line are Plymouth Puritans. The case is the reverse of the chronological order. However, Olson cannot admit the fact that the fishermen came after the Puritans. The fact that the Gloucester fishermen were preceded by the Plymouth Puritans has become the curse for America. The curse remains in the middle of the 20th century. "December 18th" reads:

It [Gloucester] is a
part of the
country now a mangled
mess of all parts swollen
& fallen
Into
degradation

(Maximus 597)

Now, what can we do, if the founding history of
America has already been corrupted by capitalism?
To answer the question is the primary task of
The Maximus Poems. Shall we search the way to
save America in the Algonquin legends which are
far from capitalist *assumptions* and have healing
power for the ego-centric people. Or, if we trace back
the ages to the "Pennsylvanian" Period and arrive
at "MONOGENE," as mentioned in "MAXIMUS,
FROM DOGTOWN – II," can we find a hint to save
America? Or shall we examine the geologies of Cape
Ann and become "a diorite man," then is it possible
to keep our soul sound enough? And if none of these
ways are efficient, should we live defeated, day by day,
cursing America?

What Maximus (and Olson) can do is, doing
everything mentioned above, to make his
own "history" and oppose the acknowledged
founding "HISTORY" of America, that is, the America
which was founded by Plymouth Puritans who craved

the union of religion and national politics.

We have a poem which shows what Maximus and Olson do. The title of the poem is "I'm going to hate to leave this Earthly Paradise." (Maximus 592-96) In the poem, Maximus and Olson walk around Gloucester through the night. They are heavily depressed but never abandon their hope. They are making their own history in the teeth of capitalist assumptions.

At the end of this essay, let us take a look at a poem which has a hope for the future. "Stiffening in Master Founders' Will" reads:

                         boys
and girls grow
long legged and don't' want to
live

in dead ceremonies
of white bulls, or surplices
of whiteness of the soul's
desire to be blind, in service
or in ecstasy. We pick

a private way
among debris
of common
wealths […]

              And one desires,
that the soul
be naked
at the end

of time
                    (Maximus 136)

This part of the poem seems just to say that "boys /and girls" who "grow /long-legged" don't like religious ceremonies described above. The "dead ceremonies / of white bulls" sound pagan and suggest a religion from an ancient age. To speak specifically, the religion may be related to the praise of Zeus who took the shape of a white bull and brought beautiful Europa away on his back. The "dead ceremonies of white bull" are related with the ancient religions of Greek and Roman myth.

The "surplices/of whiteness of the soul's/desire to be blind" states that this ecstasy of whiteness is not a good one; rather it is a harmful one which keeps young people away from the healthy growth of body and mind. The subject of the sentence ("surplices of whiteness of the soul's desire to be blind") has a hypnotizing effect. White "surplices" of the priest function as metonymy of pure soul. Thus, the sentence, with ample overtone of "whiteness" = "pureness," and "blindness" = "innocence," conveys that the religious "service" done in white "surplices" is sacred, and the "soul" is permitted to be blind to what it does not want to see.

The text reads: the "boys / and girls grow / long legged" do not want to "live in dead ceremonies of white bulls, or surplices of whiteness [...]." If the religious ceremonies of both ancients and moderns are detested by the young people, these ceremonies will find it hard to exist.

If the "boys and girls grow long legged" include the descendants of Plymouth Puritans and Gloucester fishermen, we might hope that there would come a day when the inhuman capitalism, which dates from the austere profit making Puritanism begun at Plymouth plantation, finally comes to an end.

What we witnessed by the example of Roger Conant is a history of deterioration. If these boys and girls have a simple and naïve soul like the farmers and fishermen who settled in Gloucester in 1624, they can end the history of deterioration.

Works Cited

Butterick, George F. A *Guide to the Maximus Poems of Charles Olson*. Berkeley: U of Cal P, 1978. Print.
Olson, Charles. *The Maximus Poems*. Ed. George F. Butterick. Berkeley: U of Cal, 1983. Print.

Ed Sanders

GLOUCESTER HARBOR

FORT

Stage Fort Park → 19

Cressy Beach

22
23   24
              26
                    26
         Mayflower
         Ledge   Babson
7   Ledge
    28
         25   27   25
    23

         28

         30

→ Olson ←

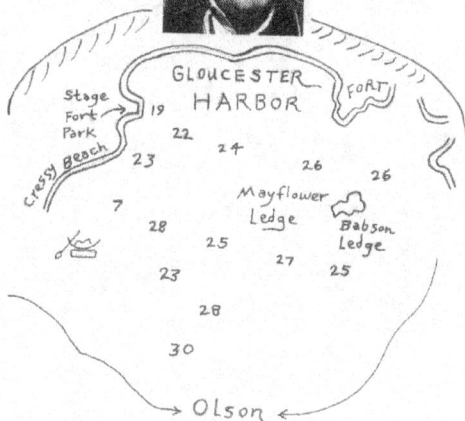

Realizing that the English & Dutch
had come ashore
            in "New England"
just as
Central & South America
were invaded
        by the Spanish, the
        Portuguese et aliae
& he was determined
      centuries later
        to focus
on the past &
the present &
            to forge
              a New America—
              Non- Imperialistic,
              Democratic
                  & for the financial
                  sharing of wealth & abundance
                  by all humans

Ed Sanders 2015

Olson Protecting
    Gloucester

"There's some good projections
that like, Christ, by 2000 the whole
idea of heritage will have been cleaned
out of the human species..."

                C.O.
            to Herbert Kenny
                Aug. 1969

as of rampant
tear-down of old buildings
            & that O considered Gloucester
                "a redeemable
                    flower"

"You can never lose to
    the City Council if your
    case is love."

    O as enviromentalist

" I even helped in that
    marsh fight over on
    Essex Ave...
    The state refused the
permit, happily, because
    of some aquarian life...
    they claimed... might
        be destroyed."

14

Edward Sanders
May 2015

Peter Anastas

Charles Olson's Call to Activism

> *I hate those who take away*
> *and do not have as good to*
> *offer. I hate them. I hate the carelessness*
>   —Charles Olson
>   "A Scream to the Editor"
>   December 3, 1965

Beginning in the late 1950s and lasting for nearly a decade, the bulldozers of Urban Renewal tore through Gloucester's 300-year-old waterfront, leveling sail lofts and net and twine manufacturers, driving ship's chandlers and carpenters out of their shops on Duncan Street and working people from homes and tenements clustered around the Fitz Henry Lane house on Ivy Court. The Frank E. Davis fish company headquarters on Rogers Street, long thought indestructible, was knocked down, and 18th and 19th century buildings of considerable historic and architectural value in the city's West End were also demolished. Only one person spoke against what had been sold to the city as a panacea for our post-war economic woes. That lone voice was Charles Olson's. Known even then, in the early 1960s, as one of the century's most important poets, Olson, who had worked in Washington under FDR, saw clearly the implications of yet another government "revitalization" program. In letter upon letter to the editor of the *Gloucester Daily Times*, he called Urban Renewal "renewal by destruction," warning the city that it was "ours to lose" if we did not stop "this renewing without reviewing," as he characterized it.

Even when they bothered to read Olson's passionately hortatory letters, many subscribers to Gloucester's only newspaper thought that the nearly seven foot poet, who walked around town with a Yucatan Indian blanket wrapped around his overcoat to keep his massive frame warm, was crazy. Enraged that the Solomon Davis house on Middle Street, Gloucester's last surviving Greek revival dwelling, was torn down by the YMCA for a basketball court that was never built, Olson composed what he called "A Scream to the Editor." "Oh city of mediocrity and cheap ambition," he charged in a letter that comprised the entire editorial page on December 3, 1965, "destroying its own shoulders, its own back, greedy present persons stood upon." Olson's imprecation would have incredible reverberations into the present.

Yet during those years of destruction and loss in Gloucester, Charles Olson was practically alone in speaking out. He took the brunt of criticism from Urban Renewal's advocates and those who were benefiting financially from a program that effectively displaced most of the families who lived along the city's waterfront (Urban Renewal quickly became a euphemism for "relocating the poor"), leaving the Fitz Henry Lane house, built in the 1850s by the eminent Gloucester "Luminist" painter, the lone survivor of the kind of downtown wreckage that had been resisted by nearby Newburyport and Portsmouth, New Hampshire. Ironically, while those two cities have suffered more gentrification than Gloucester, they have also retained their traditional redbrick architecture and the intimate quality of their inner city neighborhoods.

Inspired by Olson's example, a good deal of local activism since the early 1970s has been based on the preservation of a sense of place, a way of being in the world, an understanding that each place we live in has its own unique characteristics. Place, as Olson taught, is not only where we live, but also where we get our bearings from. Place is who we are and how we feel about ourselves, how we're anchored in the world. Place is our very identity, "the geography of our being," as Olson put it. And if we lose place, or undermine its character, whittle it away year after year through inappropriate development—chopping up neighborhoods, driving people away from the houses they were born or grew up in—we destroy the basis of our lives, if not our very identities.

As the Australian philosopher and ecopsychologist Glenn Albrecht, has written, "People have heart's ease when they're on their own country. If you force them off that country, if you take them away from their land, they feel the loss of heart's ease as a kind of vertigo, a disintegration of their whole life." In a 2004 essay (quoted in a *New York Times Magazine* article of January 27, 2010, "Is There an Ecological Unconscious?"), Albrecht coined a term to describe the condition he called "solastalgia," a combination of the Latin word solacium (comfort) and the Greek root –algia (pain), which he defined as "the pain experienced when there is recognition that the place where one resides and that one loves is under immediate assault . . . a form of homesickness one gets when one is still at 'home.'" Olson not only understood this condition, but he warned of its consequences in his letters and poems, thereby anticipating today's ecopsychology movement.

Place is topography, the look and feel of the land, the mapping of streets in a town, the complex of neighborhoods; what has been built by humans or has evolved from nature. A sense of place also includes knowing the history of where we live—who inhabited it before we did and how they impressed themselves and their culture on the land. Place includes our personal and collective history as we live daily in a given town, city or region. Place concerns the life forms we cohabit with, indeed all the biota of our environment. Place is also symbol and myth; for a single town or city, the history of its founding and growth, as Thoreau believed, can be viewed as an archetype for the origin and evolution of all places on the earth.

Considering Olson's example, it is the responsibility of writers and artists—indeed, of *all* citizens— to help those who inhabit a community to understand what forces have shaped that place, what impact its history and indigenous industry have had on its character and identity, and what must be done to preserve that identity while fostering orderly economic growth and social cohesion. For Olson, Gloucester was a *polis,* referring to the ancient Greek concept of a self-contained and self-governing body of citizens, a place of great cultural and linguistic diversity. Even given the depth of its history, no place can stand still. Like their inhabitants, places themselves are in continual evolution. The many committed citizens, both individuals and groups like the Gloucester Fishermen's Wives, who have joined forces over the years to sustain our working waterfront and the integrity of our Polis, understand this. We have never advocated for "no growth," nor have we opposed every development proposal, as some have charged. Rather, we have supported growth that we felt was *sustainable* and had the least deleterious impact on existing architectural and social structures in the community and on the surrounding natural environment, which comprises an essential dimension of place, indeed sustaining us all—the air we breathe and the water we drink, the woods and watershed areas that are so nourishing to us in actual as well as aesthetic ways, our natural ponds, and the ocean itself.

The longer Olson lived in his adopted city, interacting daily with its citizens, the more local the politics of this old New Dealer became. "I am a ward/ and precinct/ man myself," Olson wrote in *The Maximus*

Poems, "and hate/universalization" (his term for what would soon be known as "globalization."). He had the ability to peel back the layers of time in a locale, a neighborhood, a single house even, a patch of forest, a moraine landscape, to reveal the depths and dimensions of its history. Consequently, Olson helped many of us to recognize that Gloucester was not merely the oldest fishing port in America and, as such, an archetypal place of human activity; but rather that it was a living, breathing city of 28,000 interconnected inhabitants. He also helped us to comprehend that Gloucester was a continually evolving ecosphere, and that an understanding of the rich and complex ecology of one's home town and the woods and fields that surround it led to an understanding of the natural history, geography and ecology of what Olson called "an actual earth of value."

Olson encouraged citizens to study the history of their birthplace, their region and, indeed, the nation itself, as he had, through an examination of primary documents. Court papers, land transactions in probate, property line surveys, wills and testaments and Quarterly Court records of civil litigation were, for Olson, the ur-texts of history, and as significant as the land itself for reading the passage of human habitation in given places. Maps told him more than chronological histories; though when it came to the narrative he said he found more significance in town histories, written by local historians, than in the dominant works of academic scholarship.

His theory of "saturation"—that you concentrated on one place, one writer, one topic until you had absolutely exhausted it for yourself and therefore prepared yourself henceforth to take on any subject—has proved to be immensely helpful to many of us in approaching not only the study of Gloucester, but also of larger topics in literature or history.

Olson also demonstrated that by living in a book-filled $28-dollar-a-month cold-water walkup at 28 Fort Square, on Gloucester's waterfront, one did not need to possess material wealth in order to pursue a rewarding life. Olson counterposed himself and his ideas against the consumerist culture that was growing around us ("in the midst of plenty/walk/as close to/bare"), noting once, in the pages of the *Gloucester Daily Times*: "One has to have the strength of a goat, and ultimately smell as bad, to live in the immediate progress of this country."

But Olson's letters and poems to the editor are not mere criticism or jeremiad. They contain a wealth of historical, practical and ecological information and insight. Long before ecology became a household word and "environmentalists" were armed with wetlands protection measures, Olson, who had been a close reader of Carl Sauer's ecological geography, was speaking out against the filling of tidelands and productive marshes. He defined ecology, in one letter, in terms of "creation as part of one's own being," while alluding to the impact of topology on the quality of one's aliveness to the landscape, so that one could understand that to erase the land of its original forms and contours, either natural or man-made, would be to live a debased personal life on it. Furthermore, he showed how, if one is ignorant of one's own history, one's future is already circumscribed, if not blighted. And finally, he insisted in one visually stunning evocation after another— of the West End's brick and granite architecture, the pristine marshes of Essex Avenue, the mist-shrouded banks of Mill Pond—that even though much of the city was "invisible" to her citizens as a result of the daily habit of living here and taking her extraordinary beauty for granted, the destruction of even a portion of that beauty ("the brightness which sparkles still for me, a heron, some red-winged blackbirds, several hornets sweeping down the run of that small raised path") would constitute immeasurable loss, not only for those living now, but for "persons unknown to us in the future, who will never know what they have lost because easy contemporary ideas and persons dominate the land."

Taken together, Olson's letters and poems constitute a handbook for living in Gloucester in concert with her history and natural ecology. They are a call to be awakened to the morning's light as it illuminates the "rosy red" facades of 19th century Main Street, the curve of roadways on a winter's night, roads that follow still older, indeed aboriginal and animal paths across Cape Ann. They are a reminder, as Thoreau insisted, that no matter where we go on the face of the earth, someone has been there before us.

Deeply and specifically, Olson's letters are a plea that we citizens recommit ourselves to our original stewardship of the land and sea, to be held in common for human use and sustenance, not to be exploited for individual profit or gain. They are an indictment of unplanned growth and development, which was beginning to occur in Gloucester during the 1950s and 60s. They speak of unnecessary change, which brings with it resentment and anger at the loss of familiar landmarks. They speak against arbitrary decisions of government to build this or destroy that, decisions which do not include those who will be affected. And they make clear, again and again, that the loss or disregard of specific local knowledge—of the land, the sea, the people, their histories and customs—leads only to a historyless future, in which Gloucester, one of the primary cities of the earth for Olson, will become "indistinguishable from/ the USA."

Finally, it was Olson's activism against Urban Renewal, against the loss of Gloucester's historic architecture, against the filling of wetlands and all the "erosions of place," as he called them, that helped to inspire a burgeoning grass-roots advocacy on behalf of the fishing industry and the working waterfront, the preservation of Dogtown Common, now a public conservation trust, and against overdevelopment and gentrification. For in the end, this activism— citizens acting singly or in concert on their constitutional right to make their voices heard— is about the preservation of place, not only as an idea or ideal but as a real, living, breathing community: as home and biosphere. Even as I write, Olson's own neighborhood, the Fort section of Gloucester's waterfront, where marine industries and residents have co-existed harmoniously for over a century, is about to undergo dramatic change. Ground has just been broken for the development of a 96-guest-room boutique hotel, said to include "an executive suite, a bridal suite, meeting rooms with state of the art audio visual equipment and two lavish ballrooms," at the site where Clarence Birdseye invented his "flash-freezing" method for the preservation of fish. With the City's Master Plan out of date by fourteen years, this project was undertaken in a virtual planning vacuum. This unconscionable lapse in planning has allowed developers to define the city and map its future, rather than the citizens themselves, creating conflict where consensus is crucial.

Like every community, Gloucester has needed the voices of citizens like Olson to remind us who we are and what we mean, both to ourselves and the world, because living here, caught up in the stresses of daily life, our home place often recedes from our awareness. As a consequence, many of us who were born or have settled here have taken Gloucester for granted. Walking the streets daily, knowing each other, working together, even arguing together, we have been given an enormous gift, the gift of community and of the ocean that surrounds and sustains us. Even if we do not fish ourselves or our families did not follow the sea, living in Gloucester, here at the ocean's margins, we all follow the sea; and as the waterfront, which is the very heart and soul of Gloucester, stands or falls, so do we all. This is not romanticism; it's not a nostalgic yearning for the past, as some have argued—it's not obstructionism. It's who we are and what we care mostly deeply about. If we lose or abandon our sense of place, allowing Gloucester, or any other significant community where people make their lives, to become like so many American towns or cities who've lost or abandoned their identities, or been gentrified out of existence, we will lose ourselves and everything else that matters about our lives here. As Olson warned in a letter to the *Gloucester Daily Times:*

> Lose love
> if you who live here
> have not eyes to wish
> for that which gone cannot
> be brought back ever then
> again. You shall not even miss
> what you have lost. You'll only
> yourself be bereft
> in ignorance of what
> you haven't even known.

Peter Anastas
(February 6, 2015)

David Rich

A Letter to Jonathan Bayliss

Dear Jonathan,

Six years, almost, have past since you died; often I
return to our Monday conversations, our little cups of
red wine in your third-floor apartment lined with Melville and Viennese novels, the image of you consulting diligent notes on the backs of obsolete computer
punchcards, your boyish laughs, your improbable hieratic dramas about Gilgamesh only Meyerhold could
have choreographed, how I tried not to sneeze at your
cats.

I picture you in the years you knew Olson, composing exquisitely artful sentences in the syntax of gentle
humor, abandoning yourself to the "gravitational drift
of daydreams" before work, before Gorton-Pew, before
any early indication of day could mottle the night sky,
in the top-floor writing studio you called a museum,
above the Yankee cemetery. To write, you chipped
away at the stratified flint you felt your head to be, and
sought structure for symbols and key-words gleaned
from old stenographic notepads; but your structure,
you wrote, "must not be simply horizontal like a story
but also (or instead) vertical skew synchronous cycloid
cabbalistic etiological reversible and exegetical." And I
fall for your metaphor of the pre-dawn owl riding up-
drafts to earth.

Then, the haunting transcript of Olson gnashing teeth for Richard Moore's camera, calling you a "floundering fluke" who, in your "fucking book" Prologos, brought about the restoration of the English novel, the novel-as-novel, as artifice, "the first time," he said, "since Henry Fielding's Tom Jones." Olson continued, saying your opening sentence "was enough to make me sick," and that, finally, one brutally frozen night, deep in drink, he gave you what for.

Video of Don Gallo concluding a celebration of the Mass in Genoa, leading his parishioners in song, in Bella Ciao, the anti-fascist anthem, as he draws from his ancient neck the blaze of a red scarf, sent me, yet again, as I am often sent, back to visions of the Marxist oratorio on Ledge Road where you served as business manager, the tomes on sacrifice and ritual, and the pamphlets, all penned by the Red Anglican priest, Fr. Frederic Hastings Smyth. You refused to let me copy the diagram, drafted by one of Smyth's followers, illustrating the dialectical motion of economic, religious and governmental change in Europe, which would ultimately culminate in a socialist order overseen by a council of leftist bishops who are to be, as the diagram prophesies, guardians of the revolution; but I cherish the faded brown fedora Smyth wore, and then you wore, and now, smallish for me, it sits on a high shelf in the house.

Jonathan, I am writing to share with you (to share with my internal imago of you) thoughts on Olson; in my generation, disappointment in Olson, among the ones aware of him, is mounting, and you, of all people, could grasp why: despite receiving from Dahlberg a radical syllabus in 1936, of Randolph Bourne, Maxim Gorky, Marx and Lenin, Olson held to a bedrock conviction, later buttressed by Hesiod, in individual competition, what Hesiod called Good Strife, poet versus poet, fishing captain against captain. He insisted Dorn see economics, the relation between capital and labor, only as "individual experience," as radically an individual engagement as "love," and he dismissed the Marxist position of economics "as politics as money" as being "a gone bird."

I began tallying labor conflicts which took place here, in Gloucester, during the time Olson lived at Fort Square; never in Maximus does he acknowledge collective struggles waged by fishermen, longshoremen, seafood workers: where in polis is solidarity, the fight of class against class?

Laying aside Newman Shea, port agent for the Fishermen's Union of the Atlantic in Olson's adolescence, who organized a stunning confrontation against a squad of armed strikebreakers imported to Gloucester, and who envisioned a fisheries recast along cooperative rather than competitive lines, yet who strangely gets smeared with rumors of theft in Maximus, Olson omits union organizers, strike leaders, or the very fact of strikes in Gloucester. There is no talk in Maximus of strikes at Gorton's and Gloucester By-Products which, in 1960, brought harbor work to a halt for the sake, in the Gorton's case, of eight cents more an hour. No mention of fishermen who, in 1966, picketed for a pension to be funded from the proceeds of one-half of one percent of incoming gross stock. No poem for Turk Souza who, having lost his right arm on the Mary A., continued fishing thirty years and, that October, picketed with a sign around his neck: This vessel, Lady of Fatima, is unfair to organized labor. Nothing of 1968, of fishermen's direct democracy, voting to strike because three cents a pound for whiting was not a living wage.

Olson was, it should go without saying, Jonathan, no Marxist. He praised Brooks Adams repeatedly while smothering Capital in silence; yet from Adams Olson did acquire a critique of capital accumulation, one which agreed smoothly with another of his major influences, D.H. Lawrence, a critique which, everywhere, is evident in Maximus. The key to the economic and moral commitment of Maximus is, I believe, following Olson's own directive, to be found in Brooks Adams, specifically Adams' preface to the second (1896) edition of The Law of Civilization and Decay. And Olson's projective method, often picked apart for relying on exclusively masculine tropes, originates here, also in the anxieties for future manhoods in Adams' preface, and is inseparable from his critique of capital (an idiosyncratic critique of capital, however, which does not originate with Marx, nor does it necessarily reside on the left, but which is, nevertheless, a critique of capital).

Brooks Adams defines capital in his preface as surplus energies not otherwise expended, "in the daily struggle for life," energies which, he says, are subsequently stored as wealth. "When surplus energy," he continues, "has accumulated in such bulk as to preponderate over productive energy, it becomes the controlling social force." The next step, Adams claims, is that capital becomes "autocratic," redistributing energies only to those "best fitted to give expression to the power of capital."

The consequence, according to Adams, and, I believe, according to Olson, is that "the scientific intellect is propagated, while the imagination fades, and the emotional, the martial, and the artistic types of manhood decay." So long as Olson, Jonathan, following Adams, believed capital operated according to laws of thermodynamics (and believed capital to be a matter of surplus energy), energies channeled into the poem were, somehow, energies deprived of capital; and, according to this logic, a spectrum of masculinities was endangered when capital consolidated. Consequently Olson, rather than championing Gloucester fishermen or shore-workers in their collective struggles for higher wages, dignified treatment or a pension, instead celebrated the dangerous gamble of fishing itself, Adams' "daily struggle for life," which, according to this whole teleology, is the stage pre-dating capital's rise (despite Gloucester being for fish what Chicago was for cattle, monopolistic and consolidated by Gorton-Pew in 1906).

Having no use for Hegel, Olson, following Adams,

saw no ultimate socialist synthesis in the future, only social disintegration, and national exhaustion, on the far side of centralized power; this is why he delved, frantically, into historical records or archaeological field studies for past patterns of life which might be alternative to our current path (somehow seeing industrialized, capitalized Gloucester, in some ways archetypal of the Gilded Age company town, as part of this alternative). Being no Marxist, Jonathan, Olson could see no merging or synthesis of capitalism with its opposite. Running his finger along lines of history rather than lines of Hegel, he saw cyclical collapse: of the Bronze Age empires, as reliant on tin as we are on oil, crumbling into a welter of small warring nations; Romans of the Iron Age, who, from a single city-state, made a bloated empire of slavery and legionnaires; and, finally, out of the Medieval after-life of Rome, rose the acquisitive merchants, nascent corporate conquest, the Early Modern of our Modern Era.

Despite the left critiques and qualifications I raise (more could I raise), Olson remains a central poet of phenomenology under duress of the dominance of capital. The Songs of Maximus, Jonathan, I consider his clearest (even his most tender), calling out our stunned inner-workings of mind, which are breached and expropriated specifically by way of eyes. Advertising has never been, for me, the sole or even the most egregious culprit. I remain more fearful of the almost-unseeable editorial maneuvers, quietly sculpting public opinion, the news owner's sly guidance, rather than offenses of the billboard. (Why is it Olson, in his Dorn bibliography, calls "the Protestant Church," instead of the lords of finance, the real "hidden hands on the machinery"?)

The "worker on what is" is the mind, Olson wrote; the dispossession approaches completeness, Jonathan, since even our closest relationships, in our time, are mediated by corporations, and profited from. Surely Olson, in believing one could opt out, could "walk as close to bare," could withhold one's energies from capital, became the substrate poet of individual, alternative strategies, of individuals depriving capital their labor power (which, of course, begs the question of who might be in such position to do so, and whether capitalist surpluses are, in fact, required to float such renouncers). This sharply contrasts to the revolutionary position Vincent Ferrini (you remember him, Jonathan) held to, a young man in Lynn, who had no choice but to walk bare, who could imagine the exploited seizing machineries of industry and government for their own resurrection (thereby effecting the ultimate, Marxist synthesis). And, of course, Jonathan, Olson could only judge your pursuit for social-democratic surpluses, your enthusiasm for cybernetics, for Norbert Wiener, as yet a further escalating jolt toward centralized, totalized societies on the brink of extinction.

Jonathan, you were the Laurence Sterne of fatherhood during the so-called consensus after your war; your reams of metafiction, composed for your own amusement, pile picaresque vignettes into precarious edifices of symbol and semantic until, mid-plot, a linguistic glint catches your eye and, gleefully, you knock the whole crazy scaffolding down to begin fresh. You signed your correspondence simply eom meaning end of message. What can I do but, during this last half-day of the year, do the same?

eom
David (December 31, 2014)

Ammiel Alcalay

Introductory comments by Ammiel Alcalay on the occasion of Baraka's talk, "Charles Olson and Sun Ra." Fourth Annual Charles Olson Memorial Lecture. Cape Ann Museum, Gloucester, MA. 19 October 2013.

"Most recently, Amiri Baraka has lent his support to *Il Gruppo*, a gathering of writers initially convened to debunk a recent book claiming that Charles Olson was an exemplar of U.S. imperialism, and that Projective Verse was based on a military paradigm. In that somewhat macabre light—because Amiri actually published Projective Verse [Totem Press, 1959], meaning if Olson was a big imperialist, perhaps by association Amiri is a small one [audience laughter]— in that macabre light, let us without further ado give it up for Amiri Baraka."

Amiri Baraka

"That dude [Yépez] who wrote that book in Mexico, whatever his name is, saying that Olson was an imperialist, all he has to do is read that passage" in Olson—in Olson's poem (Baraka jabbing at the poem, emphasizing that this"dude" —Yépez—is clueless and just has to read "that passage")"

from
The Songs of Maximus: Song 3

In the midst of plenty, walk
        as close to
        bare
            In the face of sweetness,
        piss
            In the time of goodness,
        go side, go
        smashing, beat them, go as
        (as near as you can

        tear

        In the land of plenty, have
        nothing to do with it
                take the way of

the lowest,
including
your legs, go
contrary, go

sing

From "Charles Olson and Sun Ra." Fourth Annual
Charles Olson Memorial Lecture. Cape Ann Museum,
Gloucester, MA. 19 October 2013.

Jack Hirschman

To my Comrades South of the Border,

I realized quite early on in Heriberto Yépez's gutting of the work, image and person of Charles Olson in the former's provocative, at times, especially when writing about Mayan time, brilliant, *The Empire of Neomemory,* that a few very important things need to be understood by the reader:

Firstly, that despite what Yépez says about his not being interested in Olson but rather in the Empire which he allegedly represents, Yépez is flat-out telling a lie. He's completely POSSESSED by Olson's figure and writing technique—I'd even say my image of possession is so accurate I can go further and say that Yépez's own poetry—on the page—-reveals a profoundly intellectual influence of the man he spends a couple hundred pages condemning.

And he does this quite unfairly. I mean, even if I loathed another poet's work, for whatever reason, I'd certainly give him the least benefit of doubt by including a whole poem of his in my criticism, if I wanted my critique to be seriously considered. Yépez is a serious writer and interestingly his ideas leap around not unlike Olson's, but Yépez has a personal meanness in his pen—-something Charles never had—-that makes him twist the truth to fit a preconceived agenda of attack.

For example, I'm one who believes that the rather short poem by Charles called "Maximus to Himself" is one of if not the greatest meditative poem written in the American language since the end of the Second World War. It looks out of its great lines of simplicity inspired by the sea and regards some of the really low-blow insults that Yépez tosses out as being ultimately facile.

By not, that is, allowing the reader to experience the work, all the diatribic excoriations and diminishments —which will undoubtedly and with incredible irony put Charles on a map beyond the small cultic circle of admirers, in a way not seen in the post-Olson epoch— Yépez has pulled a fast one: like psycholog-izing the relationship between Charlie and his father Karl around Oedipal stuff when the truth that is deeper and more at the service of the whole poet was that Karl was a union man, even an organizer, and his work had a huge influence on his son's life.

The problem in part is that when Olson wrote, there was such a thing as an avantguard. But Yépez is writing in an interzone of and for the avantdead. By which I mean that "lit-biz" as it is today is just an all-get-out; avantdead=New York hustle=New York money. It's a bit like a millionaire-poet like James Laughlin who founded New Directions Press and could publish Pablo Neruda and Ezra Pound back to buck. Why? Spee freech and New York money. And with the Soviet fall and the buybuybuy of a com-puter-driven market, the creation of the avantdead.

Olson was anything BUT that. And Yépez, to fit his own fantasy of pantopia, really does a hell of a lot of misrepresenting Charles.

Yépez's thrust throughout makes Olson's poetic an instrument of imperialism. This is a major part of the book, so I guess I'll have to put away that line of Charlie's: "Black as it is, I'll keep red through it". Or all his attacks on the capitalist system in the age of consumerism.

For the record:

I've worked for the Communist movement since 1980—-actively and even militantly with the Communist Labor Party and the organization that succeeded it, the League of Revolutionaries for a New America (LRNA).

Long before I entered the CLP, when I was living in Venice, California, after having lost my job at UCLA for having led my students against the American War in Vietnam and broken a couple of State laws, I learned that Charles Olson had died. That was in 1970. A month later, I began a book of poems on the Vietnamese people and the war, based on a vodou sect in Vietnam.

The technique of that book (which was lost in the mails 18 years ago and which was recovered by my biographer in Rome, Alessandra Bava, only last December) was intrinsically informed by the Projective Verse essay of Olson's in 1950. And two years later in 1972, in the Echo Park section of downtown Los Angeles, as I began what would develop into a whole generation of poems called *Arcanes*, it was the presence in those opening pages of Charles Olson that I felt nourishing my voice because I believe that more than any other poet, Olson had opened the American "line of light" to a new generation of poets; and that's why in *The Arcanes,* the 1,000 page book of 126 Arcanes published in Italy in 2006 by Multimedia Edizione—— in the American language—-the final Arcane is "The Olson Arcane", a remembrance of the only time I had the honor of being with Charles, one afternoon in Gloucester in 1961.

Yépez takes issue with virtually every aspect of Olson's work: words like Projective are ransacked and given other meanings than the simple one Charles meant i.e., to throw forward. At one point Yépez declares that Olson's writing is cinematic, but in fact Olson detested photography, was almost old-fashioned about image-reproduction. At another point, Yépez critiques in the Projective Verse Essay the syllable and breath discourse. He puts a sexual interpretation on it, no doubt because of the influence of Frances Bolderoff on Olson at that time.

The fact of the matter is otherwise. And it didn't come from Pound or Fenollosa: the second World War had reduced the entire world to nothing, zip, nada. Human value was naught. Olson knew it. In his "La Preface" he tells it. And for a poet, what needed to be done was to take on that responsibility—-to admit the Nothing. See it from within as....the blank page, but one, now, given what the war had done, on which one

MUST THROW ONESELF in a kind of urgent, stepped-up leap of breaths and speed, not in fear of that kind of "suicide" but in an assertion of being alive in a fresh new way, And that is why Charles Olson is the poet who more than any in the two generations since the end of WW2 is the one who most brightly shows the mind and heart how to

Begin.

The key word: Begin.

The essence of what poetry is

Jack Hirschman, San Francisco, 2014

Carla, the letter b.

HERO WORSHIP: AN OPEN LETTER TO NORTH AMERICAN READERS

The View re: my Tijuana Hero, Heriberto Yépez
(and his Imperial Fantasy, Sir Charles Olson), now
strangely honoring (or not) his hero, Charles Olson,
at the June, 2015 Berkeley Poetry Conference,
commemorating the anniversary of the July, 1965
Berkeley Poetry Conference Carla, the letter b.
(or not)
Since Any Utopian Vision Should Be
Without Panel or *Place*

For Eddie D.

I write this letter from the *North by Northwest* and I come from the Middle of the Middle East and there are a few from the Global South who know me as Carla, the letter b. (once Carlo b. Carlo to you), fabled descendant of the great Egyptian-French Kabbalist, Carlo Giuseppe Suarès, but I digress. No doubt, I contain multitudes because I am always talking.

"Americans are easy pickins," I said to my friend, John, as if I could have heard it in dreamtime from my hero, Heriberto (Hache, the letter "H"), in Spanglish ("Spanglish, our double happiness, our double struggle" writes Heriberto Yépez), when John and I were driving one day, after he had picked me up at the palatial home

I worked at for a few dollars for the one known as "the kind scholar of SoCal," who had in her generosity whisked me away on a free ride, so to speak—*as I was always speaking in a language and through a name not my own*—by running me to the orange groves of SoCal to be, yes, a scholar, a graduate studies student (on scholarship) in American Literature (my thanks to her for the money for my intellectual training), soon to be schooled up North in what the poet Robert Duncan called in 1965 *The Multiversity* of Berkeley, California:

Not men but heads of the hydra
  his false faces in which
     authority lies
hired minds of private interests
   over us
     Here: Kerr (behind him, heads of the Bank of
America
  the Tribune,
  heads of usury, heads of war)
   the worm's   mouthpiece   spreads
what it wishes   its own
  false news:

I admired this Duncan for calling out the university administration and faculty of 1965 and I was pleased because I thought how far from these exclusively "hired minds" of men were we today, in 2015, since we could be men and not men, at what I had heard would be the new Berkeley Poetry Conference, which would commemorate the 1965 Berkeley Poetry Conference. I had heard that in its homage it would be different from back then: this generation of faculty and students would finally "address the gender and racial biases of the original conference, to identify poets who would help lead diverse, challenging conversations and present work that embodied a range of geographical, aesthetic, and social concerns." I was pleased by the program. Yet I wondered: I remembered the poet, Carlos Williams. I remembered in *The Times* he said "it is difficult/to get the news from poems/,but men die miserably every day/for lack/of what is found there," and I did not want to be lackluster and I did not want to be lacking and I wanted to find the real news of *The Times* behind the program and to be true to my near North American namesake, Carlos.

Yet, as I said, I was pleased. I knew that, unlike those poets in 1965, there seemed to be a pointedness of diversity in who was chosen this time, obedient to what scholars in the *North and South* have come to raise as the question of *la raza*, the race question, or the feminine man question, which was close to me, Carla, the letter b, once Carlo b. Carlo, who could be like *Carlo Giuseppe Suarès,* who believed we could go either way and could have come from the trans-lettered Q'abala Tree, or from that which I learned in my graduate school came from the Greeks, the ethnos, the ethnicity question, which is like the Palestinian question, the Negro question, the Jewish question, the Indian question, and what I had heard was the poetry of witness question and the Place of Conceptual Witless Whiteness question—I discovered there are so many questions.

And I was content, although some voices warned me about my satisfiedness: one warned me in his own language that news of diversity and tolerance could, he wrote, "occlude a culture of craft professionalism suffused with a light drab of poetic secularity": that "unlike the *unaffiliated* tribe of 'poet-seers' in 1965—Duncan, Dorn, Wieners, Olson, Spicer—this current tribe of 'poet-critics,' needing jobs of course, were *affiliated* with 'the academy,' as they continued to labor within the North American university creative writing provinces" (one of these warning shots from the mast came from the scholar, Mr. al-Quala, who would say: "We have pretty much come to the point of removing poetry from knowledge, and sticking it in the creative writing department"). And another voice warned me: "do you really think you will see visionaries here, at The *Multiversity* of Berkeley, in 2015, as some had seen seers in '65?"

Perhaps, I thought, I would. Why not? Perhaps someone would have the true vision of *una escuela de poesia*, not of people paneled up against the walls in a conference reading from pre-ordained academic categories, so unlike 1965, when LeRoi Jones (Amiri Baraka), refused to appear as a black man and asked Edward Dorn (his "The Poet, The People, The Spirit" as no category, I was told), to go for him, which he did and recalled, later:

I was not actually asked to attend the Berkeley conference of the summer of 1965, but went as a substitute forced on the organization of the conference by LeRoi Jones, who had begun to withdraw from such contact. And that's how I went as an Indian.

Strangely enough, a beautiful letter in this true "school" spirit came my way, as if from Spicer' letters to Lorca from one Alana Siegel, who called for a school of poetry in the commons which "could meet [our desires] of imagination and humanity." Her letter, she wrote, was inspired by no less than "the entire incoming class of MFA students at USC [who had just] dropped out. This act," she wrote, "inspired [her] letter, to think from the malevolence of what has been constructed and perpetuated, and the fiery individuals who left it!"

We invite everyone to reach
out to us with proposals, invitations and strategies of their
own, dreams not of creating a "better" institution, but
devising new spaces for collective weirdness and joy.

Yes, if the spirit of these fiery individuals who had "dropped out" could be captured in June, 2015, then we would no doubt hear the echoes of another time and space for poetry, as my friend Lorenzo, the love of "Jack(Spicer)'s" language, had reminded me happened in July of 1965 when the North by Northeast beach of San Francisco did cast a sort of cold eye on the compassed authority of the Multiversity of

Berkeley when "Jack" appeared there, only to drop out a month later, dead in August in the poverty ward of San Francisco General Hospital, with the sweet guitar and voice lament of Trini Lopez's lovely lemon tree song still strong in his heart, "part of Jack's essential view of the world," Lorenzo told me, "the anguish of approaching the beautiful to find it essentially untouchable, although the big song for Jack on Gino's jukebox was Quando Calienta el Sol." Ah, yes, "when the sun was hot," translated in the North as "love me with all your heart." It was, Lorenzo told me, what Jack and Lorenzo and Trini and Garcia Lorca imagined as the Real they had in common—strange, drunken bedfellows who would love each other with all their hearts and correspond "in every place and every time [where Trini's lemon could] become this lemon, or it may even become this piece of washed up seaweed, or this particular color of gray in this ocean. One did not need to imagine that lemon; one needed to discover it," but where? Under whose authority? At what "school" of the future could these things sing and correspond. Ah, yes, it could be sad and lovely with heroes in common, but I digress.

Who knows how these things wash out? I only knew that on the one day of rain in May 2015 during a decade long drought, I was forced to take cover and think: under what open umbrella of tolerance would this generation's news appear, where would the authority of their facts lie? "Well, Americans," I said, because I was always talking, "they're friendly and they don't judge and you can say anything to them, they never look back to check the facts," which is fine by me, let it be, I told John, because I was forward thinking just like them and I was remembering that fine line of the North American poet, Charles Olson (who I discovered was also at the Berkeley conference in 1965)—when I was watching a film where he had this *crazy* straight-ahead gaze in his eyes and drove off in his car which had no reverse gear, and he was asked, why do you do it, that's *crazy, man*: "Well, I like it that way: my philosophy has always been: never look backwards." Maybe that's who the austere New England poet, Robert Creeley, had in mind when he wrote:

Drive, he sd, for
Christ's sake, look
Out where yr going

Anyway, I thought, Americans—North Americans to be specific—are easy pickins, these days, particularly the liberal avant-garde ones guarding the Conferences of the Academy—we call them the avant-garde(rs). I discovered there would be no need to show these avant-garde(rs) a researcher's credentials. Take what my hero has done, the poet from Tijuana, Heriberto Yépez, who would appear at the June 2015 Berkeley conference (and then—like Jones in '65—refused to appear because of the *La Raza* question), and whose book, *El imperio de la neomemoria*, translated as *The Empire of Neomemory* by a collective of translators for a publishing venture called Chain Links, had been making the rounds for a few years to make this point so well. That point, as I had kept in my memory after reading a text somewhere by *Northern* scholars, was twofold: "1) concerning his theoretical fantasy about the imperialism behind Charles Olson's work and 2) the image North Americans want to guard and keep and project when they take in a critique of their nation's politics to appease their consciences." "This work," so write the publishers and editors (Chain Links) of Heriberto's book, "is a dismantling of Olson, and of empire, and yet it is also clearly an inside job, a book that could only be written by someone who had spent hours thinking with and through—and beyond—Olson."

Yes, my Heriberto has spent hours thinking so way beyond Olson that his thinking is beyond belief, which is fine because Heriberto can be funny at times, a merry prankster, the Yépez yapping I am proud of (who else would tell me that ""the first characteristic of the Mexican body is that it transcends colonialism; it is an unknown body" and then disappear, no longer remains, becomes unknown," which brings me to the second point about what my hero has accomplished:

he can make you dupes of your own gringo guilt and turn authoritative, academic avant-garde(rs) upside down (as one of your black Americans, not Black Mountain College Americans, Diana Ross, sings it) in the northern desire for a south of the border

189

perspective on how *anglo* poets are, as Fidel would say, *el colonialismo y imperialismo del norte*, you will accept Heriberto, in fact, you will be *simpatico* and take any Sancho's or Señor Wences's word. "In this *his* authority lies."

This is what Heriberto, my hero, has done to make you fall for him. He has done it with theory, theory even he knows has no foundation in reality:

> Right now I'm studying a master's degree in psychotherapy. The first book I reread before getting into that was The *Myth* of *Psychotherapy* by Thomas Szasz, so I won't say I believe in what I'm doing. But who cares? I don't believe in writing either. I pursue both activities anyway— without believing in them—because from a very young age I learned any praxis is better than actual reality. — The True Length of Neo-Emotionalism (A Short Story) or Heriberto Yépez: THE TRUE LENGTH OF NEO

So why would readers believe what he says about Charles Olson? He even confesses straight up: "I am not interested in Olson". How transparent can one's motives be? "Olson in and of himself does not interest me; I am interested in his character as a microanalogy for decoding the psychopoetics of Empire." My friend, the thick moustached Chiapas poet Juan Hirsch Luria, known as "*el hombre* Tzimtzum" among the bearded mountain mystics, has written me:

"Oh, yeah, Heriberto, I've heard of him. He's a fucking riot, his theories are crazy but interesting even though he doesn't know shit 'bout Olson *el polis hombre*, which is great, I mean he's fun to have at a party, for a few minutes, like he's doing shaman tricks: I mean he's got this new book on Carlos Olson that the North Americans are taking seriously, but even he knows it's a crock—"*eso some pretty hilarious caca there hombre*" I say—cause he's calling the big American Olson a sexual impotent— hitting him in his post-modern *polis* nuts, so to speak—an emissary of Empire, who lived and studied with the Mayans only to steal and freeze their sense of inhabiting multiple times into a conquistador's North American expansionist space, also suggesting he's an apologist for fascism (cause Olson, so Heriberto says,

managed to simulate that he had understood a culture by describing...how it "mixed" with his own. He simulated contact through the hybrid. He thus gave life to a new avatar of kitsch, the happy-hybrid, possibly only in the mind of the remixer. But the mix of the one and the other is fascism itself. Fascism goes hand in hand with kitsch because they are two sides of the same false coin. (The coin that pretends to be another.) Fascism is remix –

(*The Empire of Neomemory*, pgs.118-119)

And Luria continues:

You can tell from the start Heriberto is lying through his teeth. How do we know? Well, he says he is not interested in Charles Olson, in his Carlos, but the fact is he's obsessed by him—Are you joking me, he *fawns* and *fantasizes* over him. He wants to breathe through and kill daddy poet at the same time. ("Daddy, Daddy, you bastard, I'm through.") Ironically, he'll do what no academic before him could: put the big guy on the map.

Those avant private college poet boys and girls in the poet biz will eat it up in the States, where they're so repressed they want so desperately to believe anyone who will fetishize (or give him fascist eyes) and kill their father, any father, and Olson *el grandioso hombre* is a ripe target, cause he's the breath on the big dick they can't get a hold of, if you know what I mean."

From a feminine man perspective, I know what he means. It's *satisfying* how Luria reads it: what the *Norte-Americanos* don't really know about their own poets, in this case Olson, is that someone from south of the border can get away with saying just about anything and no one will check, or, as I like to put it, give blowback. You could call this their "Olsonian inertia," so Heriberto would phrase it. Good for Heriberto: if he really knows the facts of Olson's life and is ignoring them in search of a theory to prank Americans—more power to him. Or if he doesn't know the facts, which I think is more likely (I mean—why would he even bother if he just wanted to do *a parody*), so much the better, no one will be the wiser. Either way, it doesn't matter: he makes the point, and the *North Americans* look a bit guarded defending him. I applaud Heriberto. He realizes the effects of theory, which is why he can say anything, and why he confesses he won't have any sex:

> In reality things work very differently. And if sex happens, sometimes other things also happen, like kids,love. In theory-world there are no consequences / just hypothesis.
> (The True Length of Neo-Emotionalism (A Short Story) or Heriberto Yépez:
> THE TRUE LENGTH OF NEO)

"In theory world there are no consequences": I can imagine Heriberto telling you:

> I will stage you a theoretical monster, one Charles Olson, because you don't know the facts, and you want to fit the big man into the sexist authoritarian archetype you have of him ('look at how he harassed women,' you will say), and in your tolerance to accept me as a literary representative provocateur of my people as victims of literary border patrols, you will accept my facts about the evil paleface, although I'm just making them up as I go along... you don't even notice that I use the word "imperialism" without in my book referring to any

specific historical instances or events. I can create the bogey-man Olson to carry that word into his practice, I can make "projective verse" a military manifesto. I can ignore all the salient facts and relationships of Olson's life. I can say the Holocaust was fiction, Saddam is Hitler, 9/11 is Pearl Harbor. I can turn water to wine, and, well, if only not to offend me, you Americans will say 'he has a right to his perspective; we need to learn to see ourselves from the point of view of 'the other.' A win-win for me. Even the Mexican government will sponsor my trips to conferences up North so that I have the *Norte-Americanos* in crisis and lit-quaking in their books or wondering how I will stage the drunken paleface of an Olson 50 years after he staggered across the Berkeley stage.

And, if that is not enough to warn *North American* leftist anti-imperialist types of Heriberto's aesthetically rich theoretical fantasies, readers who will actually read and take seriously almost 300 pages of his riddled-with-errors, imaginary-Olson text, well, the joke, Heriberto says, is on you, refracted in a trickster text published years earlier by the same editors who may be in good faith or maybe not (who knows, their intentions no doubt were good), who printed the translation of the possibly fraudulent Olson scholarship in *El imperio de la neomemoria.* Way back in 2002, Heriberto winked at all of us—about his follies:

In recent years, I have been involved in translation-criticism experiments involving certain types of critical fantasies in which I mix real interpretation with secret self-parody or even readers'/editors' deliberate deceptions. I have succeeded, for example, in getting non-real "criticisms" (heteronomy) or supposed translations published in major magazines, or in simply developing concepts or applying points of view in which I don't actually believe, systematically attributing false quotes to real authors or manipulating data, mixing unknown fictional authors in with canonical ones — in short, considering criticism, at every point, to be fictional prose. I write fictive and parodic translation-criticism (*crítica-ficción*) without revealing it to the readers of the books or magazines that have published those essays or pseudo-translations. In many cases my use of fiction is simply indistinguishable from my true beliefs. Even though most of the time you wouldn't know it from reading my texts, I always write criticism from an insincere point of view, as a way to destroy the confidence and authority we give to the critic as a literary subject or a credible voice. (*Text, Lies, and Role-Playing*, published in Chain 9, 2002).

So there you have it: the *crítica-ficción* jig's (or is it the giggles are) up. You, dear North American *avant-garde(rs)*, who have taken Heriberto's Olson "bio that explains empire" seriously have just been had. Maybe, like me, you know this, or maybe you don't—what does it matter? (It's all good and all in fun.) You have been taken for a ride. You have just given him your authority. But the question remains: Why would readers believe what my literary make-up artist says about Charles Olson? Because he's got image conscious avant-garde(rs) from the North and the South by the balls and he knows it. As someone cool enough to be branded an avant-garde provocateur Mexican poet—I remember my niece once saying that what never stops through life, is that everyone wants to sit next to the cool kid in school—he can get away with claiming Charles Olson as a colonialist serving empire, only because the *anglos* in their tolerance are too afraid not to welcome "a Mexican perspective," their words justifying the attack by saying "Olson himself is not really the target but U. S. expansionism, in all its cultural forms, is…." Of course. Brilliant. My hero, Heriberto. A "know nothing" Olson scholar. And, ironically, if the more liberal gringos are told this could be a joke, the more sensitive they get and say, no, "he's serious, he's a serious scholar," the more they take Heriberto at his word, as long as he gets to kill their fathers, their families ("families are artificial structures" he says), through theory, as long as he plays his anti-imperial role as oppressed Mexicano. As my sister, the insistent "Carla, the double lettered b. b." said to me, "the more you get under the skin of the *North Americans* the more literal they get defending their agenda. Or, put another way, the more they're taken for a ride, the more they talk about the rights of the person taking them for the ride." Call it their inertia.

So *the jig's up*: because if you don't know the salient facts of Olson's life, which are just the opposite of what Heriberto claims and which Heriberto could secretly know (although I doubt it)—as Juan Hirsch Luria wrote me, "Heriberto is lying when he says he's not interested in Olson, since he's, well, obsessed by him, are you joking me, he fawns and fantasizes over him"—then it don't amount to a hill of beans. Even Heriberto would agree—that in a time of crisis, that when poetry is in a time of crisis—strangely, this sounded similar to one of the subjects, "Poetry and the Rhetoric of Crisis," at the new Berkeley conference—then as Mexican popular culture says: "*No he hagas pato*" (lit. *Don't make yourself a duck*, meaning, don't pretend you are not you, don't turn into a third person in order to not assume the responsibilities of knowing you are the person you accuse, don't become 3 in order to not accept you are both 1 and 2. Which is why, in time, I would plead with Heriberto in order to protect him, plead with him to take responsibility for himself, to not be "the other": "*No he hagas sitting pato, por favor*" (lit. *don't make yourself the sitting duck*), I told him. "Don't hide. Be true to your crisis, Heriberto, Hache (the letter "H" in Spanish), be true to me, Carla, the letter b.," as if our motifs could be in natural correspondence, H and b, and a musical cryptogram, so to speak, as if we could be singing under a lemon tree.

And if, as Heriberto writes, "Iraq... is Bush's way

to hide, he is the crisis itself," then perhaps "Olson is Heriberto's way to hide that he, Heriberto, is himself the crisis." Which makes me sad. To know these facts about Heriberto, who himself admits that he "came all the way from Mexico [to Berkeley] with nothing to say."

And then—this is what is funny, I mean not ha ha, but curious funny—that the time of crisis came when Heriberto really did, not in theory but in reality, wind up with nothing to say in Berkeley since he never came and refused to appear. So he resigned—he likes to do that, resign, re-sign, arrive and leave under a different name at times because of *La Raza* question: that is, because a poet of whiteness was to be paneled with him at the place of the Berkeley conference, and because she was tweeting racist "mammy" tweets among others, this had made him resign from Berkeley under his own name, which name I knew he, Heriberto, Hache (the letter "H" in Spanish), was always giving up the letters of for one reason or another (*por hache o por be*) and trying on others until he disappeared, so it was no big deal, although it was for the *North Americans* who, like me, had loved him and published him and been chained to him and read his imperial fantasy of Charles Olson with admiration, who were really sparring with him just like the poet of whiteness, he said, as if they were standing like imperial fighters in her place, so to speak, so I heard Heriberto had said, you "gringpo morons, [I am accusing] the whole system of being co-opted and being a manipulating system to promote neoliberal agents," he said, when before this day they were more innocent avant-garde(rs)—somewhere I had once heard James Baldwin saying "It is the innocence which constitutes the crime"—who had welcomed him with open arms (and whom he welcomed back) with sympathy as an oppressed *Mexicano* charging up the Black Mountain impaling the great imperial paleface, Charles Olson. Well, Heriberto believed the *Norte-Americanos* singled out this woman poet of whiteness at Berkeley to save their own ass at the conference and so he turned on them and refused to appear to be always talking and so he wanted to put them in their place, so to speak, which was ironical, because the conference was meant to place this progressive conference in place of the exclusively White Paleface one in the year of 1965, since this one was announced to be Diverse, and it was, for a few weeks, announced as just that—wonderfully Diverse, pointedly—and I was pleased, but then the day came and it was not and I was not, pleased, as me, Carla, the letter b., had wanted it to be since others, well, the diverse ones and the not so diverse ones cancelled and disappeared like bees, flew out of that place with Heriberto and did not appear because they were asking why, here, in this so-called Diverse Place & Time, where they were invited, was this Conceptual Witless Whiteness Person Pointedly not Impaled but allowed to tweet among them, and I asked why, indeed, because I was in need of answers but also wondering why was not someone sent in like the clowns in Heriberto's place, the way Jones in '65 sent Edward Dorn, why was no one coming in the spirit of the people and in the spirit of a poet like Eddie D., "and that's how I went as an Indian," he said, to talk about the Real in the Poetry Commons to talk about The Poet, The People The Spirit and Color or how that piece of lemon could become this particular color of gray in the ocean when stones had been thrown where some poets of color and some poets of no color earnestly remained and some earnestly refused to appear as one color or another one and then before we knew it and all at once some were "gone with the wind" and the *Norte-Americanos* on the one day of rain in May 2015 during a decade long drought were forced to take cover and think: "under what open umbrella would this news appear, where would the authority of our facts lie," well nowhere, since once again they were left holding the umbrella, and it collapsed, and the Place Flooded, and frankly no one wanted to have the conference day have its say, everyone was washed up, exhausted, no one wanted to put humpty dumpty together again, and the Place Flooded almost to South of the Border, beyond Houston beyond Mr. Dobbs beyond B. Traven and then, like a miracle, while so many were rescinding the waters were receding and others rose up bobbing with umbrellas and mouthing "lets re-group" so they Regrouped because the North American agents were always Regrouping and talking of *blowback* and saying "get us witnesses, back-up singers, poets of some color for "the other" poets of some color, and for the poets of no color (we only have 4 white poets remaining) who left us in this Place, drowning, get us witnesses whom we can impanel and cross talk and we'll call it, why not, Cross Talk, Color and Composition, to position our poets of color like new constellations in conversation," at this cross talk conference which took the place of the conference which had been planned it was said to "address the gender and racial biases of the original, what else, conference in the summer of 1965 but which obviously could not be because this one came with racist mammy tweets and failed as it was imagined which saddened them they said and which it now turned out to be the pointed purpose of the cross talk to amend ("the conference to end all conferences" they said) which would not be a referendum on race even as some poets had been impaled and had raced out of the place like Heriberto himself who I heard had said:

I was invited to the Berkeley Poetry Conference and I accepted the invitation (not without some personal hesitancy: am I a poet in the (North-) "American" How to participate in an event with a genealogical spirit and not contribute to its Olsonian inertia?) And amidst these ongoing questions, the Vanessa Place scandal happened and I decided I had to cancel—not because she was going to be there to save their ass because they were always cross talking—I heard him say— he, Heriberto, who I knew knew just a little history about Charles Olson—to all of Berkeley and to "the whole system" and to that whole "co-opted" place on the one day of torrential rain in May— I heard him say (and I agreed because I was always agreeing): "Frankly, my dear place, I don't want to build a dam. In this my authority lies.»

And, you may ask, how do I know these facts, *how do I*, Carla, the letter b. (who in my imaginings could in fact BE my hero Heriberto Yépez, Hache, the letter "H"), know that Heriberto Yépez really knows very little history about Charles Olson and fakes his Oedipal critique of him as *a possible joke* on the repressed gringo readers who cover their asses? How do I know, here, from somewhere north and south of a border, with only a few dollars and the hermeneutic lessons I learned from a kind SoCal scholar? That will be the subject of my next epistle in which, sadly, I talk about Heriberto, how that young man I once knew was gone, how could it be said that his oeuvre had concluded before it began, and how a little history and the promise of sex with consequences broke his inks with me and my bond with him, my hero, Heriberto Yépez, Hache, and his theory of the empire of Charles Olson.

Carla, the letter b.

A Second Open Letter to North American Readers—The View from Mexico re: how a little history and the promise of sex with consequences broke my bond with my hero, Heriberto Yépez, and his theory of the empire of Carlos Olson

I know a man who knows just un poquito de historia. This man, *un hombre mysterioso*, put in question the bond with my prankster hero, Heriberto Yépez, (of whom I wrote you in my first letter) because this mysterious man's writings made me ask: What, exactly, was my relationship with Heriberto? What was it based on? Could I be satisfied with what the North Americans call *sex, lies, and videotape*—Heriberto wrote about some of these things— rather than the Truth, particularly if the *sex*, as Heriberto has it, was not worth it? I remember Heriberto—seeming to favor the monastic life—had once written me, Carla, the letter b, who used to be the favored Carlo b. Carlo to him, and whose letters fell like leaves from the transgendered Q'abala Lemon Tree:

> ...In theory-world writing and sex fulfill you. In theory-world if I ask a girl if she wants to fuck with me, she says she needs to think about it. And so we both think about sex and that's it. In

reality things work very differently. There sex sometimes happens. And if sex happens, sometimes other things also happen, like kids, love, family, hate or orgasms. Sex has consequences. In theory-world there are no consequences / just hypothesis. (Yépez, *THE TRUE LENGTH OF NEO-EMOTIONALISM (A SHORT STORY)*

Well, Heriberto was right: sex is certainly *not* worth it if there will be children or love or family or hate— better to be in theory-world, yes—but then again, and this is where I first began to fear (and tremble) for what Heriberto demanded of me: "I'm so young," I said, "I'm so horny, I like *men and not men,* orgasms. You know what, Heriberto: Better to be excited in the real world. I—just call me *Carla or Carlo Danger*—will face the stiff consequences."

But I digress, and I will tell you of this other man, who taught me just a little history, who helped me understand what happens when an abyss is opened and we all fall in as if we thought we were filling up the space with *something* that stands for history, but does not. This *something,* sadly, happened to be the shortcomings of my hero, Heriberto—when writing on the North American poet, Charles Olson—and the facts Heriberto really got wrong about him, no joke, and how we tried to save him from his own theory of no consequence, and how another man who knew even *just a little history* could be so dangerous that we considered the nuclear option to make him vanish. But

I digress.

Many years ago, hoping to meet Jorge Borges while on a happy holiday in Argentina, I met instead the Sephardic master of contemporary rabbinical exegesis, José Faur. Faur was in the same Jewish hermeneutic "business" as my own ancestor, the Egyptian French painter and Q'abala author Carlos Guissipie Suarès who, in his commentaries, had deciphered the meanings of the biblical text *The Song of Songs*, (yes, my sexual appetite had a scriptural lineage). There are lines in these Songs which unveil a man's desire for a Shulamite, whose "rounded thighs are like jewels." Yet my ancestor, Señor Suarès, realized that the Hebrew word for "jewels," *hhalaeem*, has at its root, *hlal*, "to writhe" so that, really, rabbinically and mystically, there was some dirty dancing going on here: Madonna's Q'abala with consequences, of course. When I saw that José and I had my ancestor and a bottle of Tequilla and some dancing girls in common, I knew right then there would be orgasmic consequences.

One drunken night, I told José of my plans: to "translate" the keys to my ancestor's interpretive legacy into my own poetry—to be a critic and poet and editor and translator, in Spanish *and* in English, the going from one to the other which I still had to master. So he confessed to me this: "You need a master with a method in order to be a critic and a poet and editor and translator in Spanish and in English, so I will guide you north. There is, in the works, in *Nueva*

York, in one Señor Árbol de Almendras' office, a blossoming English translation of my hermeneutical text, *Golden Doves with Silver Dots*. It sits with *el hombre* who is editing it— you should meet this *hombre* (at least in print)."

Of course, I did not know at the time, but this man I was to meet never received credit for his editing work. In fact, it was only from José's Homeric rum-wet lips that I knew his name, a Señor al-Quala whom I imagined going as blind as a batty Borges telescoping and deciphering the dots and letters of Jose's text in the damp, wine-dark offices of Señor Árbol de Almendras. This Señor al-Quala was a Sephardic Jew whose family were refugees to America. He was a poet and a scholar, from whom I could learn English and, perhaps, *just the little history* Heriberto had forgotten.

My research drew me closer to Señor al-Quala. I discovered he had a history of tracing the political and cultural footprints of *al-andalus* in the contemporary Jewish and Arab worlds. I uncovered his translations of the great Cuban Jewish poet, José Kozer. I learned that he was a poet and scholar who had corresponded with the legendary Spanish novelist, Juan Goytisolo, who had concluded that "the spirit of al-Quala's rigor and honesty" was in the tradition of "intellectuals free of mythical, exclusivist, nationalist or religious blinkers...." And I had heard that Señor al-Quala, too, desired a young Spanish/English editor and translator, like his own Señor Árbol de Almendras who had summoned him to redact José Faur's illuminated texts, and that this could be me, so I dreamt. If only our correspondence would lead to our meeting, so I might then trust in his teaching me to be a poet, a critic, an editor and translator who could learn, well, *just a little history*, although how could I know at the time—do I digress— how ironic and fateful it was that he, this Señor al-Quala, would lead me to a book of his still to be written, informed by years of his personal and poetic alliances with of all poets, Charles Olson, the very poet Heriberto, my hero, would also write upon. Thus, you see, as I foresaw, my dilemma: my "meeting" with Señor al-Quala's Olson would have consequences—like sex—on my relationship with Heriberto's hypertextual Olson, which had its shortcomings. Sex with two images of a 6'8" Olson! Who could imagine that I would be in the middle and have to choose between them?

I want to say here, for my North American readers, because I want to be as honest and clear as can be, that when I was younger I admired Heriberto, I almost loved him, at least in theory-world. Like his rage at Olson, I was what you call short and angry at my father. I—just call me *Carla or Carlo Danger*—vented and mocked *Norte-Americanos* and played textual dress-up and wrote "pink" lettristic make-up on my black pants suits and trolled the post-ironic, cynical plots of the avantdead on the Tijuana and Oakland borders and I would, had I been an actor with a clear target, the way Heriberto had lasered his endless monologue upon his bullseye Olson, well I would have gone backstage blindfolded and picked up any prop and wielded it as a club against "the man," any man, *el hombre,* Charles Olson, Walt Whitman, Octavio Paz, it didn't matter, maybe even harangue the blind, lame master Borges with his own cane. *Carla or Carlo Danger* empathized with Heriberto's affairs and claims.

I was aligned with Heriberto's every anti-imperialistic, cynical, parodic move, even though I discovered he could, sometimes, be sincere. For example, I was so pleased he really respected the Black American innovative traditions of poetry, as he had written. They were like us.

Mexican writers understand poetic innovation and experimentalism in a way that resembles the self-understanding of black innovative tradition. As a culture fundamentally constructed to resist imperialism and alienation (and now globalization) we can't help but to be a counter-proposal to Western literature.

This, I thought, was no joke: he believed it. Two traditions: African-American and Latino—aligned in resistance: stickin it to the Western *hombre.* "I think," Heriberto wrote "we [Latin Americans] have more things in common with the African-American idea of innovations than with the 'white' one."

Yes, I believed Heriberto, but with his self-confessed satirical nature one never knew his motives, which was fine, since he was funny, and

I liked "funny," and I laughed. Like when I heard him say his clever truisms—ah, the profoundly ambivalent amoral pseudo-Nietzschean post-ironic nihilistic avantdead poses spoken in largesse— to an audience of graduate students, among whom, I confess, I sat, hearing Heriberto:

"families are artificial structures—it becomes an artificial system—it's a fake system"

"the 'united states'—it's a fantasy"

"Change is a 20th century myth. When I try to change the world, nothing happens—there's just more violence. Maybe Bush doesn't want to change. Maybe he's happy that way (audience laughs). I'm sure Bush is happy with his life. Why try to change someone who is happy (more laughter)?"

As I said, I like funny, even witty, but I also liked that Heriberto could be serious, particularly when he spoke of the African-American writers. For example, in one essay, he referenced African-Americans whom I, too, had discovered to be earnest, good poets— Harryette Mullen and Lorenzo Thomas and so on— that, I thought, well, he means it, he respects these writers, these innovative traditions. He's not joking.

Yet I dug deeper. I asked: where, in Heriberto's citings, was probably the most famous of the innovators in this pantheon of contemporary African-American writers, the revolutionary poet, LeRoi Jones/Amiri Baraka: the one figure the other poets whom Heriberto cited would honor, who Lorenzo Thomas himself would see, along with John Ashbery, as "the most influential American poet – in terms of style – of the last quarter of the 20th century." I decided to find out for myself what was up with Heriberto's omission. I gathered a little history on my own, what the Greeks called *istorin*, as to where, if at all, Señor Baraka was in Heriberto's world-view.

I found he was nowhere. And this was odd, considering Heriberto was a so-called scholar of Olson, of whom none other than this Amiri Baraka once said, referring to contemporary poets, "well, Charles basically gave us all the canvas." Baraka, who once said Olson called for "a poetry that used history and place as an engine to wrest meaning from the present. To see how now got to be now and where was it going and where had it been." And I wondered: in Herberto's imaginings, why had Olson's *barca* de Empire sailed without any departing words from Señor Baraka?

I had learned from Señor al-Quala that there was a legacy, a chain of poets, from one generation to the next, who offered us revelatory occluded histories, an interpenetration of traditions, the reading and re-reading of wildly dissonant texts in relation to each other and the news of the universe. Personally, I could locate this in my own history: my ancestor Carlo Suarès was a master of unlocking the cipher codes in the physical sciences or the plurality of universes in hieroglyphs. Señor al-Quala had seen this, had brought these traditions into the light.

I saw in his text a reference to a film by one Mr. Ferrini in which Mr. Baraka spoke of the significance of Charles Olson and, yes, as one of the people whose concerns were often ignored, I was moved to tears:

> To me, Olson's concept of the polis was just simply the idea that you had to be grounded in the concerns of the people, that the people are finally the makers of history, and that you have to be grounded in what is historical in that sense. What are the concerns of the people? Why are they these concerns? The whole question of putting the hinge back on the door. That is, trying to find out what had been hidden from us by the emergence of this new one-sided society. That was important, particularly for me being black because I knew part of that was the connection to Africa. Where are the foundations of the world from? Charles was saying, "you have to go back, you have to go back."

I researched further. I found in al-Quala's book another extraordinary African-American poet, Nathaniel Mackey, who had recalled that Olson himself knew and said in 1965 that he was "the White Man; that famous thing, the White Man, the ultimate paleface, the noncorruptible, the Good, the thing that runs this country, or that *is* this country. And, thank god, the only advantage I have is that I didn't...." Run the country, that is. Why? Because, as Mackey knew, Olson was almost alone among poets who "acknowledges"

... himself to be an heir to the corrupt power he condemns. He can own up to certain spoils the poet gathers from the workings of that power, can admit, as we have seen, that imperialism gives "a language the international power / poets take advantage of." In this we see the workings of not a clean but a troubled conscience.

Olson sometimes speaks of political power as something from which he is excluded, promoting a sense of a priori exclusion as a way of confirming his poetic vocation. But there is another side of his thought that admits that for a white male poet like himself, born in a white-supremacist, male-supremacist society, political power, relatively speaking, is a birthright from which he isn't excluded but about which he has to make a choice. A man who was once on the threshold of a political career, as he was in the 1940s, more believably speaks of renunciation than of exclusion. That is exactly what we find him doing, exhorting others to choose "to be these things instead of Kings." For him poetry is analogous to a vow of poverty, a moral act of renunciation, as he writes very early in *The Maximus Poems*:

> In the land of plenty, have
> nothing to do with it
>   take the way of
> the lowest,
> including
> your legs, go
> contrary, go
> sing

And after reading in Señor al-Quala's book these words of Mr. Baraka and Mr. Mackey, two of America's seminal poets here honoring and quoting the legacy of Charles Olson, I wondered, and I asked as if I were *saddened* by the whole affair: why did Heriberto not know this history, given, as he *said*, his bonds and correspondences with the African-American innovative traditions? Now, in secret, I started having the strangest thought—no, it was an uncanny dream—resembling how my ancestor had dreamt his hermeneutics: no longer would my ambition be to edit and translate Señor al-Quala, since a different urgency dawned on me: I needed to become desperate enough to save Heriberto from embarrassing himself with his text on Olson, so much so that I wondered: was there still time to edit his *Empire of Neomemory* post its English publication for readers who he had attracted in the post-avant-garde, to save him from his own errors, from attacks by others, if not in the real world than maybe in theory world. I dreamt, as one option, hijacking police helicopters to circle Oakland and Tijuana and unloading confetti of errata slips. I dreamt there could be other, more fateful options—only to save Heriberto from himself.

Here, then, in Señor al-Quala's book, were a set of facts about the person of Olson and his poetry and his relationships that could have shamed Heriberto's theoretical admirers, had these facts about Olson been revealed. Yet how come no one knew this book (easy to understand why *Heriberto's* countrymen would be in the dark about this text in American English but how account for the *Norte-Americanos'* visions in their tunnels)? *Es mysterioso.* I wondered: How had Heriberto done it? How had he filled this/his Olson's poetic honey head with ideal, imperial fantasies and how did everyone fall in line and say "Amen we believe that is Charles Olson's head on the stake we always thought he hung from" as if they thought Heriberto were filling up the Olson space with *something* that stood for history, but was not? No doubt, I admired Heriberto's conviction and ambition, but I was confused—because it was not history or memory but theory. I should have realized it, since Heriberto had identified "Memory and History" together: "Memory is chimera….Memory and History are identical. They are the very impossibility of control."

And I wondered: if, as Heriberto had claimed, theory world was all there was, then where was there room for memory, particularly if memory was chimera? Although it pains me to put it like this—*because Heriberto could be clever and funny and like a true poet do-shaman tricks with beautiful, even compassionate words traversing all logic*—I was astonished: *because, in the context and consequences of people's real lives, that would make theory like revisionist history to survivors of genocide.* How could there possibly be space for what Señor al-Quala had written was the "solidarity [which] remains in *the integrity* of memory, as activities and meanings become codified for general consumption?" What strange meanings around Olson and empire had Heriberto codified for general consumption, and why?

Perhaps, as Señor al-Quala had written and Heriberto and his fans thought, it was easier to deal with Olson as...a "poet [who] comes to represent the inherited weight of patriarchy or is made out to be the priest-shaman-leader of a cult [in the same, contemporary way, Señor al-Quala had said, "poets" are relegated to the "non-thinking" creative departments in the academy]." Perhaps it was easier to use his character, as Heriberto had done, "as a microanalogy for decoding the psychopoetics of Empire," ignoring reality in favor of an agenda. I wanted to save him and his defenders in the Republic of Letters from the dishonor that was about to be brought on us with Señor al-Quala's book.

And it must be understood: these were not only facts about Olson which one could look at and say, "well, look, Señor al-Quala has his facts and Heriberto has his facts and everyone has a different perspective" because Heriberto's facts really only did exist in theory world, as if he shared the stage with astronomers and was allowed to say yes "the moon is made of green cheese" or he proudly rose at a conference among African-American historians and then turned to his notes and said yes "Plantations were big open whitewashed places like heaven, and everybody on 'em was grooved to be there. Just strummin' and hummin' all day," as the young African-American Clay sarcastically said to his white female nemesis Lula in "Dutchman," LeRoi Jones's/Amiri Baraka's 1964 play. So the shame to be avoided would be this: would the "mexperimentalists" and the avant-garde or post-avant *Norte-Americanos*, be complicit in revisionist history: would we be complicit in a position difficult to defend with recourse to the mantra —"everyone has a right to his "ideas" with which "we" may not agree." Yet this is exactly what Heriberto's translators—well intentioned and more than competent—wrote in their "Notes" at the end of *The Empire of Neomemory*:

"Translation: we recognize that in writing as a collaboratively jumbled 'we,' each of us at different moments may end up seeming *to advocate ideas with which we do not agree*. (my emphasis) Translation: to sustain such discomforts. Translation: because we are dying inside this Empire."

A fantasy panatopia of empire which Heriberto says Charles Olson's writing represented—meaning, we are all dying inside the body of Charles Olson's work. How do we get out from under his yoke? No joke.

Yes, I was anti-American and counter-conquest and wanted to believe Heriberto when he said the "United States" was "fantasy," or "'America' was a comical nightmare," because we all believed we were dying inside Empire and needed to breathe and we were seduced by Heriberto's idea that Charles Olson could be implicated in Fascism and the perpetuation of American Empire.

"But, no matter how much it pained me, it was hard to believe Heriberto when I heard and saw otherwise: Here is what I heard and saw otherwise. In "This is Yeats Speaking," Carlos Olson had called *Norte-Americanos* on their own blindnesses in trying the fascist Pound for treason. Understanding just *a little history*, Señor al-Quala had witnessed an Olson who was implicated in just the *opposite* of what Heriberto had claimed: an Olson who called to the carpet the United States government's accommodation to Fascism, a government which would use the Pound trial "to establish the shadowy image of the poet through whom art's relationship to politics can be administered and cordoned off, and used as a surrogate form of debate, like a condom placed over organs of policy and their effects."

Señor al-Quala remembered Olson's words in "This is Yeats Speaking":

What constitutes "our" side is not easy to see or

state: to go no further than the term "democracy," left or center, it is too lazy, too dead of the past to include the gains of the present and advances to come. But the enemy, because he attacks, stands clear. A "fascist" is still a definition....

We have not yet shaped, because we have denied this civil war, a justice with sanctions, strong and deep enough to measure the crime. Our own case remains unexamined. How then shall we try men who have examined us more than we have ourselves? They know what they fight against. We do not yet know what we fight for....

And Señor al-Quala asked, why were the details of United States sponsorship of and links with fascist activities after the War something *which Olson alone, among the poets,* uncovered? "Our own case remains unexamined," Olson wrote, his knowledge of the "deep politics" involved a result no doubt of his position in The Office of War Information's Foreign Language Section, from which he resigned. Of these "deep politics," Señor al-Quala had written (and Heriberto forgot, no doubt, to say):

Such "deep politics," in the sense poet and historian Peter Dale Scott has defined them in *Deep Politics and the Death of JFK,* get left by the wayside again and again, especially in trying to think through the relation of politics to history and culture. While all these

Nazis were being brought into the government, Pound, a poet, was indicted in 1945, taken from Italy, and imprisoned in the District of Columbia Jail in Washington.... Never a real trial, the Pound case played an important cultural, historical, and political role. It established the shadowy image of the poet through whom art's relationship to politics can be administered and cordoned off, and used as a surrogate form of debate, like a condom placed over organs of policy and their effects. As mechanisms get jump-started by events, a series of stand-ins takes up the space of the actual, making it difficult, if not impossible, to talk about things outside their categorical function.

The case of Olson, and his concern with "putting the hinge back on the door" to the past, follows a similar course.

Through Señor al-Quala, I now noticed an irony: had Heriberto, whom I admired and who loved theory world, used Olson as "a surrogate form of debate" for an America deeply involved in the workings of empire? Had he taken the same approach with Olson which American officials took with Pound? Had he just picked on the wrong guy and used him as one "in a series of stand-ins" for American empire? Had he used him as, *cómo sex dice en inglés*, his whipping cream boy (sic)? How could I save Heriberto from the facts as Olson and al-Quala had presented them in the real world, or was this even necessary since Heriberto only lived in theory world? I asked friends for advice, and they listened so closely that they came to me with their own dreams, like my American friend, Jeff (ah, the good *Godofredo*). He said he had heard talk of Heriberto and his theories, how Heriberto thought Olson wanted "to flee from his real body" into "a replacement body," to live in language. Heriberto's vision of Olson's imaginary, theoretical co-bodies reminded him of a dream he had when in Mexico:

> I had a dream while in Mexico visiting my daughter when she was there studying Spanish. In the dream I was both me and Kafka, you know how you know that you are you but not you in a dream, yes?, and the not me who was me was Kafka. Anyway that is a minor point. The relevant moment in the dream was when I or Kafk-I said to a friend walking along side me "Max [Horkheimer], theory is a cage in search of a bird...in this case, Big Bird." To which Max muttered something like "The complexity of the connection between the world of perception and the world of physics does not preclude...misguided theorizing. I'll buy the bird seed on the way home."

I laughed—I even thought Heriberto might find it funny, since, like me, he liked funny. I dreamt Heriberto had spilled big bird's seed, waiting for Olson to fly into his cage.

I dreamt my skin sweat and I was swarmed by cicadas and actually tried to read for the first time

Charles Olson's poetry, very little of which, I now noticed as I was swatting the *psi psi* sounds of the persistent insects, Heriberto had remembered to cite in *The Empire of Neomemory*. Yes, I thought that the omission in a scholarly work of much of Olson's poetry was odd, although I was young and I respected the aging process and never wanted to fault someone for lapses of memory, *neo* or not. And, anyway, couldn't Heriberto be excused since he had already said that "memory [was] a provisional order, and "forgetting… a final substrate of the real?"

I found an Olson poem with the names of Leroy (sic} [Jones] and Malcolm (X) in it: about fathers, immigrants, borders. It went something like this:

> my father
> And I
> in the same land   like Pilgrims
> come to shore
> he paid
> with his life
> my father a Swedish
> wave of
> migration
> like Negroes
> now like Leroy and Malcolm
> X the final wave
> of wash upon this
> desperate
> ugly

> cruel
> Land this Nation
> which never
> lets anyone
> come to
> shore

The poem moved me. I felt for Charles Olson in the real world living in a nation which never let his father or anyone "come to shore." He was one of the great unwashed. I found a letter in which he said much the same to Ezra Pound:

BUT you have to deal with us Olsons... your damn ancestors let us in (AND AS ABOVE I DON'T THINK THE BATHTUB WAS SO CLEAN WHEN THEY DID). We're here. And to tell you your own truth you damn well know anglosaxonism is academicism and shrieking empire. LIFE out of Yale, CULTURE out of Princeton, and The BOMB out of Harvard.

Here was the Swedish Olson rejecting empire, seeing himself just like the gringos saw Heriberto and his people, a wave of unwashed wetbacks on the *frontera*, which made me wonder why Heriberto had made him the poetic front man for empire and had written that...

Olson's verbal talent and his patriotic imaginary made him a perfect fit as an intellectual bureaucrat of the American propaganda machine....

On the one hand, he continued to idealize the United States immigrant, an idealization he inherited from his father, and on the other hand his gift for nationalist rhetoric and his talents as a writer made him a key employee in the apparatus of petty propaganda. (Yépez, pg. 36)

...when I saw that he did not idealize anyone, at least not according to what he wrote in *The Post Office*:

My father valued America, as immigrants do, more than the native. I'm not sure it's a good thing. It wasn't, in my father's case, as this trouble he got himself into will show, though for me his fascination with the story of this country was fruitful, as it sometimes is, in the second generation American. There is a sentimentality about the freedoms of this country which none of the bitterness of poverty and abuse will shake in an immigrant. My father had it, at least up to this trouble I write about when the government of these States so failed him he was thrown back on that other rock of the immigrant, his foreign nationality organizations.

I discovered Olson was not Heriberto's nationalist naïf romanticizing the immigrant. He actually rejected both the government of the United States (the so-called rights it bestows on a citizen, which his father lost) *and* the immigrant societies which act as cocoons and into which an immigrant is tempted to withdraw when he gets rejected by his adopted country. He imagined that, had his father lived, and with the help of Gloucester, his local community, the *polis*, "he might have seen his "struggle" *outside* both Sweden and America," outside the lines both demarcated. I wondered: how much did he sound like Heriberto at the *frontera:*

At the *frontera*, the Other is repelled. Both sides of the línea are rejected like two magnets of the same sign which only force could keep together, in so far as as soon as we allow them to operate according to their own rules, the separation is violent [...] If the apparent theme is bidirectionality or symbiosis, the deeper theme, in contrast, is incompatibility" (Heriberto Yépez, "La hibridación es un engaño. El significado real del arte fronterizo," *Made in Tijuana*, 2005).

Yes," the deeper theme... [was]incompatibility," Heriberto wrote, and he was right and thus, ironically, resembled Olson, "the patriarch," the ancestor, the son of an immigrant father who had foreseen someone like Heriberto waiting on both sides of the *línea*, whose struggle could not harmonize the "*happy hybrid*"— Sweden and America. I was in a dilemma.

I noticed that Heriberto was more like Olson than I thought, than even he thought. I remembered my friend, the mountain mystic, Juan Hirsch Luria, saying: "Well, Heriberto claims he is not interested in Charles Olson, but the fact is he's *possessed* by Olson— Are you joking me, he fawns and fantasizes over him. He wants to breathe through and kill daddy poet at the same time. It's what keeps him *alive*. 'The energy transferred from where [Heriberto] got it,' from the poet Charles Olson, to himself. It's what I call for Heriberto the return of the repressed or, in his case, projective verse!" And it was already clear, given what Juan had said, that Heriberto was so obsessed by "his father" that he wanted to keep him alive by projecting his presence onto his own. I dreamt Heriberto starring as Ray Milland helplessly screaming *Estoy Vivo! Estoy Vivo!* in Tijuana's film version of Poe's "The Premature Burial." I dreamt trying to pry him from his self-made coffin. And I remembered the night Juan had secretly whispered to me how the seductive, crazy logical leaps and sinuous syntax of Heriberto's language felt as if it aspired to the breath of Olson's prose, but I could not tell. Regardless, it did not make my dilemma any easier. I wanted to breathe for my hero, Heriberto, who could not breathe for himself.

Here was the dilemma, which cut three ways— it pained me to say—as failed homage, parody, scholarship. I knew, of course, that Heriberto was a provocateur who could get cranky and intimidating, but I wanted to please him. I wanted to save him from the real world from which he had deported himself. He was, after all, the philosophical poster boy *por nihilismo* among the young. So I wondered:

first, if he was so much possessed by the father, Olson, to mimic him, to fantasize over him, then how keep this homage a secret from his fans, who had, through Heriberto, savored their retribution on the master. Obviously, his so-called dismantling of Olson was a front and not very persuasive, particularly if I, with minimal training at the hip bone of a kind SoCal scholar, could see through the disguise and figure out he actually loved the master of empire, Mayan or otherwise. I give credit where credit is due: this interpretation of mine was revealed with Juan's help and a little bedtime reading of *Herr* Dr. Freud's Hamlet: "*mein Sohn* (*mi hijo*, my son), you only tear down what you can't stand (next to)."

Second, I had already determined, in my first letter, that this was no calculated fiction to deceive *Norte-Americanos*. My dilemma was how to conceal my disappointment in what brought me to Heriberto in the first place: his prankster—ism. It was clear his book on Olson did not reach the standards of Yépezian critical satire or what he named *crítica-ficción* (I articulated this in my first letter), particularly since I, again someone with not much hermeneutic practice, could see right through it, even before the scholars who had defended it as "serious scholarship."

Finally, and this greatly saddened me about how far my hero, Heriberto, had fallen, *The Empire of Neomememory* was now perceived as failed scholarship, theoretical over-determinism, revisionist history from an oedipally challenged grandstanding *nihilismo*, and it was being defended "up north" as "the view from Mexico," which hurt me because it absorbed his people in this whole affair and which I, after discovering from Mr. al-Quala's *a little history*, had to confront. I heard the oppositional, threatening bloggers, one in particular, a follower no doubt ensconced in Mr. al-Quala's anti-academicized cells, directly addressing Heriberto:

Heriberto, if you believe "the post of Olson is evasion, the evasion of the history of the imperialist civilization to which he belonged," then the post of you, Heriberto, is *invasion*, the invasion of the academy of the avant dead civilization to which *you* belong. *Hoy usted* will be hoisted by your own petard.

The logic was so tight in its conviction that I imagined, in my loyalty to Heriberto, ways to silence Mr. al-Quala and his crew, to tighten the screws on them, who knew much through *a little history*. Ironically, Mr. al-Quala was *the mystery* man who would lead the life of me, Carla, the letter b. or Carlo Danger, or at least the life I had really wanted to live, since to everyone he would meet he would stay a stranger. He had hordes scoping him, but it didn't matter—he tried to fly under the radar. Still, the young North-Americans—avant and post-avant-garde(rs)—had to take a stand. They had been seduced by the disarming elegance of Heriberto's language, by the lispy playfulness of his Plathian ethos—Daddy,

Daddy, you basard (sic0), I'm through—by the anti-
Norte-Americano pose of this *hombre* from Tijuana, a
literary province, mind you, certainly not the capital
of Mexican letters—who was going after the imperial
posse from Up North. It was clear the al-Quala posse
had to be stopped. A little history had taught me
that the only way anything would be settled was that
someone had to vanish, and why not Mr. al-Quala.

The set-up, in theory, was perfect: Yes, it was true,
forces were at work to belittle Heriberto, but they
were not imperial forces. Instead, they were as anti-
American as he, but in reality not theory. One of these
was Mr. al-Quala, who had a little bit of a shadowy
history himself. He knew much, too much. More than
that: he remembered too much, and the few people
behind him remembered what he said, even in an age
when "memory was chimera." In the past, and in reality,
he had been the target of a North American Academic
Campus Watch. He appeared on lists of dangerous
tenured professors who were framed as anti-American,
pro-Palestine, anti-Israel in an article straight out of
the government's vigilance handbook, a piece entitled,
"Poetry, Terror, and Political Narcissism." If he were
scoped, I thought, it would be the campus conservative
watchdogs who would be suspect. No one would look
our way.

Further, because we all knew that for Heriberto
"memory is chimera," and "memory and history
are identical," Señor al-Quala was what Heriberto
hated most, an archivist of knowledge, whose work

remembered—no found—what had been lost, no doubt like Olson's. I'm sure that, according to Heriberto, his work, like Olson's, was "an expansion towards the other, towards the fusion with an appropriation of the other....Olson [who] devours the other, [who] swallows the other into his own life, and likewise, is devoured by his prey...." For Olson, Heriberto had said, "erudition is a hoarding, defined by banking and expedition" and, thus, empire. And so, Señor al-Quala was implicated as well. And since Señor al-Quala was already suspect, I wondered, mostly because of my loyalty to Heriberto who taught me the meaning of irony and renunciation of change in a post-Mexican era void of truth, did my Heriberto devotees and countrymen and young *Norte-Americano* avant-garde(rs) have access to stockpiles of whatever the post-avant nuclear option might be in order to make Señor al-Quala and his cells and their kind of "little history" disappear, not in theory but in fact. (We imagined stockpiles of disappearing inkwells mushrooming in a blogged down age which welcomed hyper-tolerant equivalents of flat earth theory?). What if he and his writings were "disappeared," lost, never to be found? The only question remaining: would it be fission or fusion? Heriberto, I knew, would have favored fission. For Heriberto's sake, there would be no dialogue with history, no false coherences, no textual fusion of cultures, which for Heribeto meant "fascist remix." For Heriberto, there would only be fission unleashed in one lit quaked city by the Bay.

But it was not an option, practically or theoretically,

and the thought vanished as soon as it was triggered. The problem was deeper, since Heriberto's writing would still be present for any future gardener to unearth. In the end, my dilemma came down to this: The Heriberto I loved had become a disappointing fraud, at least in terms of his knowledge of Olson, but the fact was I loved him precisely because he had always been a disappointing fraud. He acted the literary roles expected of him, as Mexican critic, or so he said, "performing a kind of role-playing as an author within a specific culture (in this case, the Mexican Republic of Letters)" He wanted, he said, to build "communication between our two cultures through imaginary entities and lies." His "fictive criticism… was part of a *diálogo diablo* (to use Groussac's image) on the periphery of Latin America, a *devilish dialogue* or *diabolical dialogue*, a sort of wanna-be experimental cross-cultural setup which [could] accomplish much more than more serious academic approaches." He was, to an extent, a little like me, when I worked for that kind SoCal scholar, when I hoped my skills would gain me entry into a dialogue with her)—on the heroes and anti-heroes of literature. For example, I would have treasured, like the recovery of a trunk full of manuscripts, a dialogue with her about my other hero, my distant cousin, Carlos Bernardo Soares, who once said:

I am the sort of person who is always on the fringe of what he belongs to….. Everything around me is evaporating. My whole life, my memories, my imagination and its contents, my personality – it's all evaporating. I continuously feel that I was someone else, that I felt something else, that I thought something else. What I'm attending here is a show with another set. And the show I'm attending is myself.

Hearing my cousin, distant though he was, it hit me: my bond with Heriberto had always been as a person on the fringe of what I belonged to—since there was really nothing there with me and Heriberto, except in theory, as there was really nothing there with Heriberto and Carlos Olson, except in theory. Curiously, perhaps this was the way Heriberto would have wanted things to end: to be represented by a fact-less biography that explained nothing. So be it. Let him rest, resign, not be, be himself. He had tried to be authoritative and I had tried to save his image, but something else had to happen to rescue him from his "post-Mexican" identity. Maybe he had to become post-Heribertoan.

In fact, one could even say that in my separating from Heriberto, my hero, he had actually succeeded, because I came along to free him from his scholarly follies in order "to destroy his authority as a critic" (these were Heriberto's words, not mine), which he never liked, or to save him from creating yet another irony to hide his vulnerability in the real world... (I never did that, people heard me confess I almost loved him). But if only a little history was what it took for the memory of Heriberto to be, well, chimera, then,

231

so be it, our bond would have to be broken. Yes, of course I was saddened that it had all come down to a vanishing act in order to break my bond, that it all had to go up in smoke, so to speak. But what else could I do but let him go? As he once wrote, and as every one of us knew, "all this role-playing was utterly nihilistic and boring." And certainly my loyalty to Heriberto, no matter my disappointments, would not allow someone else to just come along willy-nilly and use his irony against him, which is why, plain and simple and not in theory, he had to go before anyone came back for vengeance, lest some stranger come along one day and say with pleasure

"Heriberto, hoy, usted will be hoisted by your own petard."

Michael Boughn

Olson, Empire, and the thinking of America
for Peter Q. who knows how it feels

"Spurning the clouds written with curses, stamps
the stony law to dust, loosing the eternal horses
from the dens of night, crying: *Empire is no more!
and now the lion and wolf shall cease.*"
—William Blake, "A Song of Liberty"

"Do you think that men who have enjoyed the
blessing of liberty will calmly see it snatched
away?"
—Toussaint L'Ouverture

"You have no power over my body, neither can you
do me any harm . . ."
—Anne Hutchinson to John Winthrop and the
General Court of the Massachusetts Bay Colony,
1637

"This country is without hope. Even its garbage is
clean . . .."
—Jean Baudrillard, *America*

America's reputation – a quaint word in relation to
a long history of violence, conquest, and exploitation
– beyond its own shores has been in tatters, at best,
in much of the world for a very long time. At "best"
because tatters at least retain some mark of the
imagination of a time of first distinguishing energies

that promised a new world. At worst, with no tatters to invoke that original thought, America is simply a force of destruction, cruel and violent, obliterating everything unique and dear in the world, everything of value. It relentlessly degrades the human world into a homogenized, universal *culturemarket* made up of billions of *consumers,* indistinguishable except for their market profiles. It transforms the physical world into a never ending river of commodities to feed that market, while virtually enslaving whole populations to produce them. Jean Baudrillard's observation after his cross-country U.S. jaunt pretty much sums it up: "[America] is a world completely rotten with wealth, power, senility, indifference, puritanism and mental hygiene, poverty and waste, technological futility and aimless violence . . .." While the rest of the world finds this obvious, inhabitants of the United States seem almost aggressively oblivious to it. They continue to repeat the mantra that America is *the best* and that the world should pull up its socks and get on board the modern-democratic-hygenic express because lots of goodies are to be had, including its bestselling products, *democracy* and *liberty.* And so they drive into the sunset, one hand on the steering wheel, the other on a Big Gulp, ignorant of the fact they are the shimmering embodiment of an esoteric doctrine known as *exceptionalism.*

It's all tied up with the thinking of *America,* a word with many different registers of meaning beyond the definition of the United States. The U.S. is a juridical/

political entity occupying part of the northern half of the western hemisphere. Geographically, America is that whole western hemisphere, north, central, and south, pole to pole. One of the habits of U.S. Americans that annoys the other half billion inhabitants of the hemisphere is their assumption that *America* belongs to them, dismissing the rest of us.

But *America* means more than geography. It is an idea, and like all ideas, has a history, though it tends to get lost in the political uses to which the name is put at any given moment. And the history is entangled with other ideas and events. The idea of American exceptionalism was active by the time of the Revolution, central to the commitment of U.S. leaders to spread Republican democracy around the world. It has been the focus of academic debates over the meaning of America since about the time Charles Olson published *Call Me Ishmael,* his first address to America, in 1947. Shortly after that, the premier issue of *American Quarterly*, published by the University of Minnesota, hit academic library shelves across the U.S. Both events were part of a moment in which the active thinking of *America*, as well as America's thinking, opened into a range of attention and authority it had never before been granted. The founding of The American Studies Association followed from *American Quarterly,* which then became its voice. The initial issues of the magazine reflected a strangely naïve intellectual patriotism, probably because the university was still mostly the preserve of privileged men, and they thought of America as . . . well, theirs – which it was. Describing his essay as "another chapter in the history of American patriotism," Merle Curti, in that first issue proposed to make a "contribution to a larger study of the images that peoples in other parts of the world have held of the United States." It was, he said, to be a scholarly contribution toward persuading the world of America's exceptional status as the avatar of modernity.

The American Studies Association changed over the years along with the university that nurtured it and the object of its study. In the 1960s, with millions of people in the streets fighting for civil rights, the promised but still undelivered equality, and the end of the war against Viet Nam, the thinking of *America* shifted to a decidedly more critical mode. Universities began the transformation from finishing school for future leaders and managers of the nation to job training centres for the middle class, and their moral focus shifted from anxiety about preserving Christian culture toward an attention to social justice. The curtain of modernity's consensus was pulled back, exposing the "white man" operating the levers of illusion. Authority (which is always problematic in America) fragmented and American Studies became a centre for theoretically engaging the *exceptionalism* that justified an America of deceit, oppression, aggression, greed, and exploitation.

Olson's book was part of this conversation. Developed from his Master's thesis at Wesleyan in the 30's (and his salvaging of Melville's dispersed library) and fine-tuned during his coursework with F. O. Matthieson in the American Civilization program at Harvard, *Call Me Ishmael* entered the growing world of Melville scholarship and the American Studies context it was part of, loudly announcing its difference. Rather than the smooth, seamless rational coherence of sanctioned scholarship, *Call Me Ishmael* unfolds into ir/regulation, dis/continuity, in/coherence. Olson's thinking forays beyond the forms and usages of academic scholarship, radically reassessing Melville, his novel, and the America it addressed. Just as *Moby-Dick* announced the end of the rule of the "empire of forms," *Call Me Ishmael* assaulted the authority of a scholarship divorced from the blood and tears of an actual world. Rather than symbol and allegory, Olson disclosed the economics of the whaling industry as Melville's narrative measure of American expansionism. Whale oil, he argued, was the black gold of its day, and whaling the economic engine of the emerging American economy and its drive for world hegemony. Ahab's maniacal assault on the white whale mirrored America's drive to consume the world, a drive founded, he proposed, on cannibalism.

Most people track American exceptionalism to John Winthrop's 1630 sermon, "A Model of Christian Charity," written on the *Arabella* just offshore from the new world. Winthrop appropriated the biblical reference to a "city on a hill" shining as a beacon to the rest of the world to describe the new colony. That part comes at the end. Most of the rest of the document justifies social and economic inequities as

God's will and establishes rules about money. It lays out the nuts and bolts of managing the new colony, from how to mediate disputes over ownership to the proper controls on lending and borrowing. While the authorizing ground of the document remained the Puritan covenant with God, the rules governing the order of the community were made up, based on perceived and projected needs of the community in a strange new land. It established the order of the new society with a text. Sacvan Berkovitch points out that Winthrop did not appeal to family or to utopia, the traditional models for community: "What is displaced is both visionary (a medieval utopia) and actual (familial, communal, and geographical origins). What comes into place is broadly modern: a community written into existence by contract and consent, through a declaration of principles and rules that bend tradition to legitimate a venture in colonial enterprise." Establishing the founding order as textual mattered. Although it would have horrified Winthrop to think so, this gesture projected modernity beyond theory into a world without foundation and opened it to the antinomian implications of liberty.

America was unique in that regard. Even Baudrillard admits it: "America is the original version of modernity. We are the dubbed or subtitled version." That may or may not be exceptional, but it was the first time anyone had established the order of a political body outside the authority of tradition or the transcendental. Upping the ante in 1776, the further act of founding proceeded to incorporate the intellectual pyrotechnics of the Enlightenment in its textual ground. A nation based on philosophy as it was being written by men. It was barely imaginable, a cosmological earthquake. People got excited.

> A vision from afar!
> Sound! sound! my loud war-trumpets, and alarm
> > my Thirteen Angels!
> Ah, vision from afar! Ah, rebel form that rent the
> > ancient
> Heavens! Eternal Viper self-renew'd, rolling in
> > clouds,
> I see thee in thick clouds and darkness on
> > America's shore

William Blake's "Song of Liberty" addressed the thirteen rebellious colonies as angels. In the collective imagination of that moment, *America* opened into an unprecedented range of relational possibilities and prodigalities that, as Blake said, rent the ancient heavens, leveling hierarchies, further democratizing the authority decentered in the Reformation.

Baudrillard goes on, "I cannot help but feel [America] has about it something of the dawning of the universe." The dawning of the universe is serious business. He doesn't specify what it looks like, but it doesn't matter because the dawning itself is the point, just as the textuality is the point in Winthrop's founding sermon. That figurative first light connects to an old American thinking about newness, beginning, discovery, illumination, about an opening beyond the imposed cruelties of the known, in the discovery of a new world. Baudrillard's response registers the perennial American sense of liberty from the drag of history—which is both its doom and its promise. If the founding texts result in a couple of centuries of bad faith, they also crucially preserve the possibility of rewriting the real.

Charles Olson's artistic engagement with America begins with the proposition, "I take SPACE to be the central fact to man born in America," the opening sentence in his first book, and arguably that engagement never ends. He came by his interest honestly. America was an unprecedented opportunity for Europe's poor in the 19th and early 20th centuries. It offered them land, independence, and the right to participate in the redistributed sovereignty of the Republic, none of which were available to them in Europe. But it also promised the liberty not to participate if you didn't want to. After a couple of thousand years under the thumb of one monarch or another, with one bunch of Cossacks or another riding through your hovel, it sounded pretty good, even if there were no guarantees. To the young Olson, growing up in the heart of the old, revolutionary United States surrounded by its monuments and battlefields, America looked like a promise realized. Olson, the son and grandson of working class immigrant families, lived the promise, attending some of the finest schools in America's and realizing what his family could never have achieved in the old class bound structures of Europe.

At Worcester Classical High School, Olson was exposed to the wild outburst of American writing from the mid-nineteenth century. It balanced his classical education and added depth to a sense of a particular America of value. Emerson, Hawthorne, Thoreau, Fuller, Dickinson, Whitman, and Melville challenged the authority of the empire of literary forms (and the thinking that is tied up in it), opening up new paths for writing and thinking in the same American space that Olson shared with them. Emerson was the heart and mind behind it. Olson chose his essay, "The American Scholar," as the subject of his commencement address at Wesleyan. Emerson's call to arms arose out of anxiety about the timidity of American art and scholarship in rising to its unique occasion and producing something new from within its own specificity. The fact he thought it possible testifies to the emergence of some new spirit, one he identified with "the near, the low, the common." At the same time he proposed that American specificity as transitive, not thinkers, but thinking, which he in fact did. His condemnation of "Genius" that "leaves the temple to haunt the senate or the market" and his passionate, demonstrative love of the process of thinking, its surprising activity, rather than its accumulation and possession, left a deep mark on Olson.

Olson's landmark essay, "Projective Verse," folds Emerson's "Man Thinking" into what Olson calls the projective, which entails not only a mode of writing, or even, as Olson states, a stance, but a whole new propositional real in which such a stance can find traction. Emerson recognized the unfolding (American) real in the loss of bedrock truth or law, say its *textuality*. Mood displaces knowledge, or at the very least, casts it in its tone, leaving knowledge with no truths to grasp. "Gladly we would anchor," he wrote, "but the anchorage is quicksand." It won't just *not* hold you; it will swallow you.

Baudrillard notes the other side of the modern: "America ducks the question of origins; it cultivates no origin or mythical authenticity; it has no past and no founding truth. Having known no primitive accumulation of time, it lives in a perpetual present." That lack of accumulated time leaves serious conversation in America a difficult event. Without history, or at the least some common representation of the past besides cartoonish "myths" of shared turkeys, felled cherry trees, and perennial victory there is no given common ground from which people can begin to address each other and their situation. On the other hand, these same conditions entangle and shape Emerson's moral perfectionism, his prescient tropological morality with no foundation in law. Contradictions multiply without any hope of rectification. Contra-diction, against the word which is the hope of rectification. The idiocy of liberty.

Emerson leverages that in "Self-Reliance" into an uncompromised (groundless) but easy engagement with the emergent world, "the nonchalance of boys who are sure of a dinner," he calls it. Olson finds confirmation of that new cosmology in Whitehead's process philosophy. He works out one of its implications is his critique of inherited prosodic modes (what used to be called the "laws of verse") as the enactment of nostalgia for a non-existent ground. Prosody is cosmology, the rhythm and rhyming of knowing. And the freedom to shape prosodic form outside the given, to make something new, something that equals the real itself, becomes entangled with the thinking of liberty.

Liberty is an uneasy thought these days, largely because of the duplicity that surrounds it. After nearly 350 years of slavery and its aftermath in Jim Crown, segregation, institutional lynching, and programmatic lethal violence by police, the word rings hollow. When the U.S. waves the flag of "liberty" while laying waste to anything that gets in the way of its expansion, liberty becomes a joke, the punchline in a story about how to distract a sucker while you lift his wallet and leave him stranded. It's an old American tradition that goes back to John Winthrop, again, and his "Little Speech" in 1645. Responding to a failed attempt to challenge his power to manipulate elections, he contracted liberty into two opposite possibilities, predictably a good kind and a bad kind. Outside the law, he said, liberty involved acting like an animal: it was "common to man with beasts and other creatures. By this, man, as he stands in relation to man simply, hath liberty to do what he lists." A certain terror lurked in the shadow of that "lists," one where animals and humans listed to do unspeakable things with each other in the tenebrous reaches of the wilderness. Winthrop called it *natural* liberty, gobsmacking "Nature" and exposing it to all manner of assault. The good kind, logically consistent with his gender theology, offered an early taste of later Orwellian developments. You were to use your liberty, Winthrop said, to freely give up your liberty, like a good wife freely gives over her liberty to her husband when she marries. He called this patriarchal travesty *civil* liberty.

Anne Hutchinson was decidedly not a good wife in Winthrop's terms. She adhered to a religious view called antinomianism which held that salvation was through grace, not works, and that the Christian was therefore not bound by moral law. More importantly, she refused to stand down when ordered to do so by Winthrop and the General Court. She was not only a bad wife, she was disobedient. Her lawlessness extended from the theological to the domestic in a defiant assertion of her liberty from the authority of the Court. In a show trial that could have been a model for Stalin's judicial monstrosities, Hutchinson was condemned as a heretic and an instrument of the devil, and, along with her family and followers, expelled from the Bay colony. They were later killed in an Indian attack on Long Island. In a journal entry dated September, 1643, Winthrop coolly described the massacre of Hutchinson and her family and blamed it on them for having "cast off ordinances and churches."

Winthrop was surely thinking of his old enemy and her antinomianism when he distinguished between lawless (animal) and lawful (human) liberty. Susan Howe has proposed antinomianism, that lawless liberty or liberty from the law, as an elemental American mode of thinking. She locates its beginning with two exemplary women: Hutchinson and Mary Rowlandson. In Hutchinson's case, the lawlessness is obvious. The intellectual repercussions flow out of her arcane theology into issues of the liberty of conscience and freedom from mental law. Her antinomian belief in a covenant of grace was in many ways less threatening than her refusal to recognize patriarchal law on any level, her open defiance of Winthrop and the General Court.

Rowlandson represents a different face of lawless. Captured by Indians during King Philip's War and held in captivity for 11 months before being ransomed, Rowlandson wrote about it in a strangely conflicted narrative. Howe proposes that Rowlandson went through a kind of reverse conversion that lurks in her text beneath the socially required rectitude of her surface narrative. She "excavates and subverts her own rhetoric," Howe points out. In Howe's reading, Rowlandson's captivity ex-posed her to the world beyond the pale and she tasted the openness of the wild as she relished the taste of raw horse flesh. She was set on "a forced march away from Western rationalism, deep and deeper into Limitlessness, where all illusion of volition, all individual identity may be transformed—assimilated." This image embodies Winthrop's nightmare of natural liberty.

Not actually antinomian in the religious sense that Hutchinson was, Rowlandson's narrative still resonates with the potential freedom opened in the entangled encounter with American space. Even the implicit duplicity of its form, a captivity narrative containing a secret conversion narrative, speaks to the lawlessness just past the frontier. Antinomianism and liberty, although not the same, both question the law and stand disobedient before Winthrop's Court and his "civil liberty." Antinomianism involves opposing the *nomos* which is grounded in custom and usage. Liberty, which comes out of the Latin *liber*, refers to the absence of restraints and is connected through *liberalis* to a sense of generosity. Liberty is perhaps more open in the prodigality of its possible dispositions than antinomianism, which it provides ground for. While Howe persuasively locates Emily Dickinson's work as antinomian (although not in the root, religious sense), it can't be separated from the discourse of liberty. Liberty, Emerson said, is "the doctrine of poets." They both fed into what Howe calls "the primordial struggle of North American literary expression."

In that expansive sense, antinomianism and liberty are two aspects of the thinking of writing as they affect the determination of the next word, how the form-ing of language is engaged, whether left to a habit that evades thinking or a rule that tries to abolish death, or embraced as an articulating entanglement with the finitude of an im-perfection of emerging. Howe points to the radical textual formations of Dickinson's fascicles, and argues that the ongoing (male) editorial regularizing of her wild, eccentric forms indicates the war in American culture on antinomianism, especially on women writers. But Emerson is still everywhere in Dickinson's thinking, from his proposal for an American art and writing that "announces what no man foretold" to his call for writers to "upheave nature." Dickinson's challenge to the authority of thought and form answers that call. So do Whitman's invention of a new line and his challenge to laws of Christian moralism. And Thoreau's (and Emerson's) invention of a new form of writing thinking, formerly known as "philosophy." If liberty masks U.S. hegemonic violence with a razzle dazzle phantasm, it is no less this thinking of freedom among words—among many other things. Its nature is extravagant and prodigal in its im-perfections.

What Howe calls "the erasure of antinomianism in our culture" is related to what others refer to as "Empire," at least as it metaphorically entails the eradication of difference and the elimination of resistance to its totalizing power. It came on hard and fast in America, lurking in Winthrop's rhetoric as much as in the land grabs and outbreaks of violence against the natives. Francis Jennings argues each of the English colonies was a mini-Empire, and they quickly embraced genocide against their new neighbours, playing one native tribe against another, as they began their relentless expansion across the continent. In 1638, under the command of Captain John Mason, English colonists allied with Narragansett warriors bypassed a military engagement with Pequod warriors with whom they had provoked hostilities, and instead attacked the Pequod village at Mystic where they massacred over four hundred undefended and unarmed children, women, and elderly. They then beat a retreat from the enraged Pequod warriors who had been waiting to fight them elsewhere, till they were resupplied with arms and men and turned and destroyed the Pequods. They wrapped up this initial exercise in genocide by systematically tracking down survivors, executing captured males, and either killing the females, giving them as gifts to allied native tribes, or selling them as slaves in the West Indies. The United States emerged from the blood and enslavement of the Pequods, while arguably America was lost.

Melville, so crucial to Olson's thinking, tended to identify his boats with *America* and to load their names with significance. The Confidence Man's steamer is "Fidèle," *faithful*, but also *believer*, a poke at the gullible, self-deceived Americans living merrily in the midst of an unacknowledged horror. *Pequod*, the name of Ahab's ship in *Moby-Dick*, is even more pointed, identifying that floating, catastrophic America with its founding genocide, as if America was lost before it was ever found. Olson confronted the loss early in the poetry: "About seven years | and you can carry cinders | in your hand for what || America was worth," he stated in *"Captain Christopher Levett (of York),"* written in early 1958.

It was a complicated kind of loss, tied up with Olson's complex sense of the destructive energies unleased by the failure, as Emerson had it, to actually discover America. Slavery figures in it. Although slavery was not the defining institution in New England that it was in the South, Olson does address it in "Letter 14" in story of John Hawkins, a slave trader, and the way in which his "business" was part of the failure of America. Christopher Levett, on the other hand embodies a particular relation to the world, the *stance* Olson also writes about in relation to John Smith, and Hawkins' father, William, who "made friends / among the natives, Sierra Leone / or Brazil // And had such honor / in the new places . . .." Smith, another early European explorer, was significant for Olson because he "was doing it for one of the very first times. It's a different thing, to feel a coast, an ancient thing this Smith had, what men had to have before Pytheas." This timeless mode of encounter or entanglement with the wild/world (which Olson translates into his sense of the *postmodern*, groundless and projective) is also initial, not as time factored, but as always further.

In "The Kingfishers," his meditation on change and renewal, Olson identified it with the ancient Mayans, one of the first first people in America, who, Olson says, because of that, were "hot to get it down the way it was." That "hot to get it down the way it was" points to the same attention Olson found in Pleistocene man, inventing the human in the shadow of the retreating glaciers as they encountered another "new world:" "A new world took form," Carl Sauer, Olson's favourite geographer, wrote, "developing the physical geography that we know. The period was one of maximum opportunity for progressive and adventurous man." That relation remains a potentiality, waiting to be activated. For Olson, two factors figure in the loss of that *ontological adventure* for the Maya, and presumably ourselves: the slippage of attention, a kind of epistemological failure or laziness, and "that other conqueror we more naturally recognize / he so resembles ourselves," Conquest is one name for it, Ahab's mad drive to kill the whale, a compulsion Melville connected to the fear of death and modernity's controlling subject.

Olson ran smack into it during his war time work at the Office of War Information. Whatever lingering sense he might have nursed about the moral purpose, as Ken Warren has it, of the United States as a force for world historic change, ended in his recognition of the decidedly immoral political machinations and maneuvering for post-war expansion and world dominance that gripped the state apparatus from the front lines to the upper echelons of the U.S. government. It was a deeply transitional moment for Olson in which his belief in the transformative power of American democracy, a belief grounded in the fight against fascism which saw him justify certain political choices he later rejected, came crashing down. It wasn't abstract. He was in the thick of it, making calls as the ground shifted under his feet. His plan to reenergize the practice of democracy in the U.S. ran head first into the new Praetorian Guard of Coca-Cola marketers imported from Madison Avenue to sell the war and prepare the ground for post-war American expansion into the ruins. Olson tried to carry on but he was censored into silence. Rather than write ad copy to sell American hegemony, he resigned:

> (o statue
> o Republic, o
> Tell-A-Vison, the best
> is soap. The true troubadours
> are CBS. Melopoeia
>
> is for Coke by Cokes out of
>
> Pause

Soon after, he severed his ties to the Democratic Party which had been grooming him for leadership. At Berkeley, he referred to this moment of renunciation as his "only advantage:" "And in fact, the only advantage I have is that I didn't [run the country], so I can stand here among men who have done what I couldn't do, can't do."

It not only marked the end of Olson's political career, it marked the end of any lingering illusions about the value of the U.S. as moral agent of change. It marked the beginning of his resistance to U.S.

violence in all its forms, from international economic and political conquest, to cultural homogenization and commodification, to the continuing war with antinomianism, to its aggressive national narcissism and ignorance of anything other than its meagre fantasy of its own "exceptional" self. In recent years, Olson has been accused, among other things, of complicity with something called Empire, and specifically American Empire, a notion that circulates widely, although often without much attention to questions about "Empire's" composition, or even its existence. Mostly these days, "Empire" functions as a metaphor for evil rather than as a descriptor of an actual organization of power. The threat of the Imperial Death Star replaces discriminations of sovereignty in discussions of the role of the U.S. in the world.

Once the metaphorical fog gets cleared, questions surrounding sovereignty and Empire are multiple and complex, and related to the United States, seem to come down to two possibilities: there is an American Empire, but it differs from historical Empires because it developed out of a new form of sovereignty; or, however brutal the push for U.S. hegemony may be, there is no American "Empire" because, as Walter Scheidel argues, "[i]n the most fundamental terms, the capitalist world system is not conducive to archaic flavors of territorial conquest, and it is hard to conceive of any realistic scenario that would make long-term violations of this principle appear both desirable and feasible." This is not to deny the fact of U.S. hegemony, its military interventions, its control of international monetary policy, and its self-interested manipulations of trade. But it does clarify how metaphorical distortions obscure rather than illuminate actual dynamics.

Complexities aside, the analyses point to sovereignty and law as determining issues in understanding American power. They are relevant as well in understanding Olson's relation to America. A specific unprecedented form of sovereignty developed in British North America. It differed from the forms of sovereignty that other European colonial powers imported to the new world, mostly because the various European colonizers came with different intent and encountered different worlds.

In Mexico, the Spanish found a world they knew well. The enormous, complex, oppressive Aztec bureaucracy with crowns, priest castes, nobility, warriors, and slaves, was much like home. Sovereignty was centralized and hierarchical. The Spanish, who were there for the loot and not settlement, took over by replacing the ruling class. They allowed large groups of Aztecs (mostly nobles) to gather for religious ceremonies. In the midst of their worship, the Spanish massacred them, as Pedro de Alvarado did at the Main Temple of Tenochtitlan in 1521. Once the seats of power were vacated of Indians, the Spanish invited themselves in and started running the place. One of the first orders of business, learned from the Christian destruction of pagan religions in Medieval Europe, was razing Tenochtitlan and building Mexico on its ruins.

The natives were subjugated and used for labour.

For all its own particular horrors, British North America differed. English colonizers did not import monarchical sovereignty. Instead they invented a new form based on their particular (though not exceptional) American experience. While Spain transferred its transcendent, monarchical sovereignty to Mexico, in British North America, as Michael Hardt and Antonio Negri point out in their book, *Empire,* republican sovereignty developed in relation to the settlement of a new kind of space. Sovereignty was reorganized as a "universal republic, a network of powers and counter-powers structured in a boundless and inclusive architecture" While the "imperial" nature of this sovereignty is a subject of contention, its revolutionary structure isn't. As Haedt and Negri argue, "Against the tired transcendentalism of modern sovereignty, presented either in Hobbesian or Rousseauian form, the American constituents thought that only the republic can give order to democracy, or really that the order of the multitude must be born not from the transfer of the title of power and right, but from an arrangement interior to the multitude, from a democratic interaction of powers linked together in networks."

Hardt's and Negri's new form of power is *made* rather than *bestowed* from above. Grounded in text, it established the common, the ordinary as the metric of the real. De Crevecoeur described this state (of being) in *Letters from an American Farmer.* Travelling through

the New York countryside, he observed there was no
" . . . hostile castle, and haughty mansion, contrasted
with the clay-built hut and miserable cabin, where
cattle and men help to keep each other warm, and
dwell in meanness, smoke, and indigence. A pleasing
uniformity of decent competence appears throughout
our habitations." He goes on to condemn both the
horror of slavery and the savagery of the frontier, so
he was no dewy eyed *Americainiste*. But he recognized
something new when he saw it.

The founders of America, at least the ones who
wrote about it, had no problem with Empire. In fact,
only in the last century has Empire taken on the
associations with evil currently identified with it. For
those early Americans, the Roman Empire, with its
republican structure, stood at the pinnacle of civilized
accomplishment. Besides providing artistic and
architectural inspiration, it became the basis of their
program for using republican democracy as a control
apparatus. Whether this meets the requirements to be
classified as *Empire* is less interesting than the new
reality it introduced to power. Rizomic, to invoke
Deleuze, rather than vertically rooted, it operates
through networks. It "is constructed on the model
of rearticulating and open space and reinventing
incessantly diverse and singular relations in networks
across unbounded terrain," as Hardt and Negri observe.
The experience of "liberty" (which everywhere
infused the European air in those days, informing
new thinking about self, authority, nature, economics,

government, knowledge, time, space, and God) is at the heart of it. Sovereignty, Hardt and Negri point out, is "affirmed, different from the European one: liberty is made sovereign and sovereignty is defined as radically democratic within an open and continuous process of expansion." This new phenomenological space is "free of forms of centralization and hierarchy typical of Europe" and European colonial ventures such as Mexico. It *opens* into a new potential experience of *spacetime.*

The question of space and time and self – what are they, what is their relation, how are we to think them past the now defunct Cartesian schema – are central to Olson's thinking in everything he wrote. While they are Given within any specific epistemological framework, they are always propositional. From Pliny to Copernicus to Newton to Einstein and Bohr, the proposition changes with the epistemology. Mythic time, circular time, empty time, shopping time, bent time, all appear in the shifting focus of mental lenses' concentration. *Spacetime isare* opening, foraying, furthering past any settlement of the moment. Olson's SPACE as he engaged it in the beginning of the Melville book registered a new opening. This opening rends, shattering the integrity of feudal time with its hierarchy of sacred days and the divine wheel of their turning. It spreads out, opening as/into liberty. Connected to the hegemonic narrative of the American "frontier," it implicates liberty in the removal of the indigenous populations not just from sight, but from memory.

Hence what Melville in 1855 in *The Confidence Man* called the metaphysics of Indian hating in a chapter wryly titled "Containing the Metaphysics of Indian Hating, according to the views of one evidently not so prepossessed as Rousseau in favour of savages." Melville identified that hypocrisy as a poison in the heart of the United States, then in the midst of the so-called Indian Wars, the final genocidal wave that eliminated the aboriginal populations from American space. There can be no frontier if people live on the other side of it.

But the frontier was only one fact of the *opening* as millennial event. Contradictions erupt in irreconcilable openings beyond that. In Mexico the native population provided slave labour for the extraction of wealth and so continued to provide value to their conquerors. In the U.S. native populations obstructed expansion and so were erased from the U.S. national cultural memory other than as figurative elements in adventure narratives or moral allegories of Rousseauian primitivism. The moral corruption of the removal of Native Americans from their land marked the birth of the U.S. in hegemonic violence. But the opening of the liberty of this new space was/is multitudinous and ontologically contradictory. While the *otherness* of the natives was encountered as an obstacle and eliminated, the otherness of the spacetime beyond the "frontier" became part of an unprecedented, determining experience of the real. Octavio Paz locates it as a contesting otherness beyond the range of psycho/

sociology, that wild that Mary Rowlandson discovered-herself-in-and-in-herself, the dark matter of the world that abides within the common. Paz, in The Labyrinth of Solitude, has it as the other side of reality and links it to poetry's openness: "[A]lthough tied to a specific soil and a specific history, poetry has always been open, in each and every one of its manifestations, to a transhistorical beyond. I do not mean religious beyond: I am speaking of the perception of the other side of reality." The complexity of any moment and its irrepressible prodigality of meaning and sense is not a matter of history (a chain of causes leading to) nor is it reducible to a moral consistency. It is an otherness that fills without ever quite fulfilling while opening into the transhistorical and transnational.

The hegemonic drive of U.S. expansion across North America continued occupying space so it could expand its networks. But *otherness* is entangled in the emergence of this new mode of sovereignty. Liberty's sovereignty is extravagant, not allegorical. The potential spills out in-filtrating minds with potential form. Olson's SPACE is one fact of it. Large, he says, and without mercy. That SPACE and the colonizing, genocidal space of Manifest Destiny both emerge in liberty's opening. But whereas Manifest Destiny concluded at the edge of the continent, Olson's projective opened into the wild that is excluded from the United States, that "natural liberty" that resists any fore-closure of form in the name of law.

Olson's attention always focussed on the big

picture and what it revealed about the otherness of our circumstance. His sense of the violent historical conflicts between peoples was contextualized within his thinking of migration as the constant fact of the human: "Migration in fact (which is probably / as constant in history as any <u>one</u> thing: migration," which, he goes on, "always leads to a new center." He is careful to keep its feet on the ground, specifying it as "the pursuit by animals, plants & men of a suitable / . . . environment." On this scale, movement problematizes moral judgement since the forces involved are inhuman. Humans merely move with and within the inevitable and perennial process of the world. Olson took one of his leads here from Brooks Adams' proposal that two great migrations (or, as Adams called them, Expansions) defined Indo-European history. Driven by revolutions in metallurgy, radical new technologies, one extended from 3500 BCE to 284 CE (during which time assorted empires rose and fell to the delight of later historians), and the other from about 1000 to 1897 and after, which included the invasion, conquest and settlement of the Americas by Europeans and the birth of several actual Empires.

In "Bibliography on America for Ed Dorn," Olson contrasted this view of the orders of time, which he called millennial, to what he here called "history," another word that takes on multiple meanings in his thinking depending on his focus. Here humanism defines "history" both in scale and content. It gives coherence to the (made-up) story of the human. The millennial opens into movements on a scale that renders the human insignificant. Migration is constant. Flows of peoples up out of Asia and across what became Europe; flows of "three huge drives from the Polar North down on to the three legs of the future;" flows across the Bering ice bridge and down the west coast of America in one violent displacing wave after another, none of which invoke moral angst. Once history is out of the way the millennial reveals a world of perpetual motion that, if you push it back to Pangea, as Olson does, is as much geological as it is biological – or, say, a determining order of cosmos, a prevailing habit of the real. Flows slow and seem to stop, but the movement just shifts scale, new centers form, from micro to macro, and around them stable structures. Then migration becomes centralized, hierarchical, and stable till some other wave or expansion, some multitude on the move, crashes into it and the pieces scatter.

Which was not much comfort to the Pequods, or anyone else who found themselves in the path of that juggernaut out of Europe in the 17th and 18th centuries. Olson didn't have much to say in the poetry about that dimension of the English encounter with the existing inhabitants of the place he otherwise writes in such detail. It is a painful absence in some ways. But the issue was not out of mind, although as usual for Olson, his emphasis was on understanding the big picture rather than expressing moral judgments. After the publication of *Call Me Ishmael*, he planned out a companion volume to be called *Operation Red,*

White, and Black which fell through when he was unable to find funding. The proposal, included in the *Journal of the Charles Olson Archive #5*, began with the judgment that: ". . . the reality of our past has been so laid over by the moral assumptions of the writers that we know nothing of our selves. I see in the Indian, white and Negro life here on this continent a series of FACTS which, if properly selected, juxtaposed and coldly told, will together make a FABLE mostly now unknown." Earlier in 1947 he had noted: "or *Open* here 6. CABEZA DE VACA: and turn back to Indians via de Vaca's medicine, so that you catch all three—White, Indian, Negro at once." And then, in a further note: "But the first fact is that the American Indian has made a life out here in North and South America a hell of a lot longer than we whites: 10,000 years ago he came, and from that time to 1500 A.D. (Anno Diaboli in his reckoning) he was boss here."

Olson's recognition of 1500 as Anno Diaboli for the native Americans clarifies his sympathy for their circumstance, but his thinking focusses largely on the wandering de Vaca who briefly crystalized an exceptional American reality, a new world in which the Europeans and African took up the mode of life of the Native Americans they encountered in their walk from sea to sea, integrating their knowledge of this place, and living together peacefully. Having become a healer using Native knowledge and techniques, de Vaca and his companions were followed by increasingly large numbers of Indians until they encountered Spanish conquistadors in northwest Mexico. The new world ended when the Spanish gathered up de Vaca's native followers and sold them as slaves.

Olson's SPACE connects only tenuously with these "historical" issues. It occurs in an another register of phenomenological encounter, the event of the open, "free of the forms of centralization and hierarchy typical of Europe," and entangled with the process that Emerson points out goes on day and night. Both spaces exist simultaneously in an irreducible complexity of contradictions without hope of resolution. Olson's SPACE announces the end of the space and time of Euroamerican modernity and the various dualist apparatuses they enliven through their separation. It embodies sheer physicality entangled in *spacetime* as the projective emergence of the real.

In that sense, Olson's understanding of "history" opens into a new dimension. Writing about Thoreau in *The Senses of Walden*, Stanley Cavell observed that ". . . America exists only in its discovery and its discovery is always an accident; and to the obsession with freedom, and with building new structures and forming new human beings with new minds to inhabit them; and to the presentiment that this unparalleled opportunity has been lost forever." Given these terms, the SPACE Olson claims in *Call Me Ishmael* names the encounter with the open as discovery. It is the open as specifically discovery after the closed, well-trodden spaces of Europe. Olson does not propose this "space" within the modern discourse of binaries, and specifically a binary involving *time* and *history* as a series of causally related moments. He moved beyond that Newtonian box of containers that hold the world hostage to their discrete mutually exclusive measures. Time, then, not as a succession of discrete moments; not even as relative or dilated. Space not as an empty container; not even bent or contracted. At Goddard College, Olson was explicit that it "is rather quantum physics than relativity which will supply a proper evidence here, as against naturalism, of what Melville was grabbing on to when he declared it was *visible* truth he was after. For example, that life, that light is not only a wave, but a corpuscle. Or that the electron is not only a corpuscle, but a wave." Time, then, as an aspect of emergence, a dynamic field of space/time/ matter.

Locked in the duality of time and space, imperial culture defines its spatial control in terms of temporal achievement, as the apex of a narrative of history. For Western Europe this has meant an attachment to the achieved form as a confirmation of the cultural perfection of Empire. An Empire of forms dictates the limits of the imagination in compulsory hierarchies of value and excellence, and within that, recapitulates the forms of Empire. Time becomes the time of power within the forms of Empire. They are varied and ubiquitous in every register of life and thrive within the closure of the fantasy of perfection. Olson's SPACE reopens time into the im/perfections of liberty's prodigal entanglements. Space doesn't *contain,* it *opens,* is *opening*. The shifting forms of sovereignty mark the change of Empire's achieved time of consolidated conquest into the restless networks of American hegemony, an entanglement that also yields the times of Charles Mingus and Thelonious Monk, of Louis Zukofsky and Robert Creeley, of Philip K. Dick and Diane Williams. The entanglement of resistance. The entanglement of restless imagination. The entanglements of the prodigality of the opening, the projective.

Taking his lead from the mathematics of Bernhard Riemann and the process philosophy of Whitehead, and locating them in the strangeness of Bohr's quantum physics, Olson wrote the end of a world of discrete objects and temporal progression and in its stead wrote world as a dynamic creative manifold emergence. Olson moves beyond modernity's space/time binary and establishes a continual dynamic of manifold congruences that express the open where *spacetime* emerges as/in liberty, undetermined. We are returned to discovery as event, our event. In this sense there is no "history" in *The Maximus Poems*. Even with their incessant attention to the minutia of America's past as he located it in often obscure texts, the past does not unfold in a meaningful order. There is only the discovery of this moment in all its richness.

The texts remain, remnants of the multiplicity of *spacetime's* diverse emergence. And the texts, when deployed within another text, begin to embody *spacetime* in complexities of relation that undo past-present-future – say, on Madam Gross's lawn in *Maximus* III.135, *wherewhen* a world is played as on strings: "even as that fox / was seen by me, that what // I offer you as now out of my right eye myrtle / flower and leaf are loud by presence solely // and gone in the thought." Even as Olson is decentered by the fox, objectified, recomposed in that entanglement of forms of being, he is (dis)located by the mass of recorded details of events that are gone but that are here, that *are here*, as related in the previous three pages of the (not) past that are entangled in the moment on the lawn. The event is discovery, surprise, projective, liberty.

In the 1960s and into the 70s, resistance to the brutality of U.S. hegemonic violence spread around the globe even as the two superpowers competed for dominance: the armed struggles in South East Asia; the anti-Soviet movements in Eastern Europe; the anti-colonial wars in Africa, the anti-imperialist and anti-capitalist student uprisings in Europe and the Americas, black militancy and self-defence in the United States. The disciplinary orders of the hegemonic powers began to lose their hold.

Various forces intersected in this event in the United States: the spread of the counter-culture, the New (and elements of the Old) Left, the women's movement, various identity groups, artists and writers of many stripes, and ordinary people who, confronted by Selma, My Lai, and Kent State, had had enough and were energized to fight for justice on multiple fronts. This world-wide mass movement included diverse modes of resistance. Because of its nature as *mass*, no single interest or issue, no single demand or orientation, no single strategy or tactic, dominated. It opened forms of life into the multiplicity of their actual composition in resistance to the law's containment. One of its prods was the continued thinking of liberty and of a lost or undiscovered America.

Among writers and artists living and working in some state of resistance to the hegemonic apparatus, *The New American Poetry 1945-60* became a significant provocation, offering a focus for one range of resistance to what Hardt and Negri call "the mass refusal of the disciplinary regime." Barney Rosset's Grove Press, which published *The New American Poetry 1945-1960* in 1960, was active in opposing U.S. hegemonic ambitions on multiple fronts, both political and artistic. In addition to the *New American Poetry 1945-1960* and books by Bertolt Brecht, Samuel Beckett, William Burroughs, Alain Robbe-Grillet, Leroy Jones/Amiri Baraka, Jean Genet, Michael Rumaker, and Octavio Paz, Grove published Regis Debray's *Revolution in the Revolution* (1967), *The Autobiography of Malcolm X* (1967), *Fidel Castro Speaks* (1970), Franz Fanon's *The Wretched of the Earth* (1967), *Che Guevara Speaks* (1968), and numerous other works that were central to the resistance. Because of this the CIA targeted Rossett and the press in Operation CHAOS, its domestic espionage program.

Part of the hegemonic program of the U.S. involved monopolizing information dissemination, maintaining control over the representation of its violence and the resistance to it. *The New American Poetry* was implicated in the push to resist that control. Every word assaulted U.S. expansionist violence and the empire of forms central to its cultural control mechanism. Olson's essay, "Projective Verse," became a celebrated articulation of an opening beyond that constricted real. If the book raised the American flag (or a fragment of it) on its cover, it was to recall the myth of revolutionary intent entangled in the nation's confused thought of itself. To undertake to rewrite America remains an American thought if only because the original claim was textual. The poets in *The New American Poetry* did that repeatedly, leading to a proliferation of radical poetries that quickly spread beyond its initial limited (mostly white male) contributors to include a diverse uproar, including, as Ammiel Alcalay has pointed out, Ann Charters, Hettie Jones, D.H. Melhem, Joanne Kyger, Diane diPrima, Susan Howe, Rosemary Waldrop, Alice Notley, Eileen Myles, Ann Waldman, Daphne Marlatt, Kathleen Fraser, Diane Wakoski, and many others. One of the centers of that uproar, one of its provocations, as Amiri Baraka confirmed, was Olson's projectivist poetics, which in his autobiography, Baraka described as a bible that gave "voice to feelings I had about poetry and about society."

But Olson's sense of politics extended his poetics beyond the poem into the meat of the day with which the poem is entangled. As Baraka went on to note, ""What fascinated me about Olson was his sense of having dropped out of the U.S." At the Berkeley poetry conference in 1965 (in the midst of the international political uproar), Olson introduced this politics into the mix, resisting the institutional inertia that threatened the conference itself with becoming integrated, despite its content, into the disciplinary regime, in this particular case, of Literature.

In 1962 at Goddard College Olson announced that poetry readings had become a bore: ". . . it's become a performing art, you feel as though you have an audience, and as if you're supposed to do a concert or something." His unease had to do with the loss of poetry's contact with the immediate, the revelation of language's naked entanglement with liberty. The projective, not as an idea, but as exposure, the dynamic of exposure and the refusal of the disciplinary regime that emerges to limit its opening by commodifying it, institutionalizing it. In Berkeley, after several days and a series of conventional readings, Olson took to the stage with a bottle of Cutty Sark and famously held it for over three hours. It was a stunning – performance is the wrong word – present-ing, presencing, a revelation of mind at work in all its flawed but beautiful amplitude, an offering of contact, or as Al Glover proposed, a spontaneous recital in Avicenna's sense of ta'wil as the revelation of the soul's ascent.

Olson came to Avicenna through Henry Corbin's work in 1960 in the essay, "Cyclical Time in Mazdaism and Ismailism." Three days before his event while in Berkeley, he read from Corbin's *Avicenna and the Visionary Recital* regarding the two groups of terrestrial angels: the ones on the right who know and order and the ones on the left who act and obey and who are the titular spirits of writers. The Avicennan notion of the ta'wil, according to Corbin, "usually forms with tanzil a pair of terms and notions that are at once complementary and contrasting. Tanzil properly designates positive religion, the letter of the Revelation dictated to the Prophet by the Angel. It is to cause the descent of the Revelation from the higher world. Ta'wil is, etymologically and inversely, to cause to return, to lead back, to restore to one's origin and to the place where one comes home, consequently to return to the true and original meaning of a text." Olson's Berkeley ta'wil stunned an audience waiting for a poetry reading (including Olson's friend, Robert Duncan, who famously walked out in the middle of it). It was a marvellous moment in which Olson's politics/poetics came together in a stunning "admission:" "You know—I'm the white man. I'm that famous thing, the white man. The ultimate paleface. The noncorruptible, the good. The thing that runs this country, or that is this country." Olson's revelation comes in the midst of an admission of a sense of inadequacy and jealousy: "And I sat in Gloucester, suffering, suffering! That the world had been captured by Allen and Peter and Gregory, and in fact, their own master (like my Pound), Burroughs."

Coming from someone considered by many to be one of the most powerful men in the world of contemporary poetry, a patriarchal figure, this confession in itself was deeply political in its self-exposure of the poet's weakness and humanness. It was a public outing of the duplicity of the image of implacable masculine authority. He went on to mention Gregory Corso's reading in Buffalo earlier in 1965, and revealed one source of his sense of inadequacy to be his "protected" existence: "I never read in a coffee house in my life. I never spent an hour in jail." The statement about being a white man follows, which in this context, seems to be a confession of his understanding of the way his "social identity" (big white male) has negatively limited his experience of the world, including access to funky reading venues. He goes on: "And in fact, the only advantage I have is that I didn't [run the country], so I can stand here among men who have done what I couldn't do, can't do," acknowledging his rejection of that powerful role in the post-war Democratic party, and his solidarity with those who never had the choice.

Beyond that, the implications call attention to Olson's growing consciousness and acknowledgement of the emerging democratic diversity of voices rising in America (and around the world), the eruption of contradiction into the body politic, out of the resistance to American hegemony (many inspired and provoked by *The New American Poetry 1945-1960*) and his desire to stand among them. It announces his awareness of the inequity at the heart of American life. A few minutes later he responds to Ed Sanders, saying, "I don't like that first Maximus. I never have, because of that goddamn principle which is phallic—I mean, it's like a phallic image. And, you know, that's a lot of bull shit . . .."

Around this time Olson was composing the Maximus poem that begins, "I have been an ability—a machine—up to / now. An act of 'history', my own, and my father's, ..." He goes on to identify his own immigrant past: "my father a Swedish / wave of / migration after / Irish? like Negroes / now like Leroy and Malcolm / X the final wave / of wash upon this / desperate / ugly / cruel / Land this Nation / which never / lets anyone / come to / shore . . .." If it is a "filthy land," a "foul country" where "human lives are so much trash," (the eternal disappointment) it is also still potential – the United States does not, in other words, control the final determination of America, that endless potential of liberty: "And an end to Hell / — end even to Heaven / a life America shall yield / or we will leave her / and ask Gloucester / to sail away . . .."

Works Cited

Adams, Brooks. *The New Empire*. Cleveland: Frontier Press, 1967.

Alcalay, Ammiel. *A Little History*. Ed. Fred Dewey. LA and NY: re:public / UpSet Press, 2013.

Baraka, Amiri. *The Autobiography of LeRoi Jones/Amiri Baraka*. 2nd ed. Chicago: Lawrence Hill Books, 1967, p. 282.

Baudrillard, Jean. *America*. Tr. Chris Turner. London and NY: Verso, 1988 [1986].

Belgrad, Daniel. *The Culture of Spontaneity: Improvisation and the Arts in Postwar America*. Chicago: U of Chicago P, 1998.

Berkovitch, Sacvan. "A Model of Cultural Transvaluation: Puritanism, Modernity, and New World Rhetoric." Diss. City University of New York, 1997. Trans-Atlantic Conference. Harvard University. Web. 23 Feb. 2011. <http://web.gc.cuny.edu/dept/renai/conf/Papers/Keynote/Bercovit.htm>.

Blake, William. "America: A Prophecy." In *The Complete Poetry and Prose of William Blake*. Ed. David Erdman. Garden City NY: Anchor/Doubleday, 1982.

Cavell, Stanley. *The Senses of Walden*. Chicago: U of Chicago P, 1992.

Clark, Tom. *Charles Olson: The Allegory of a Poet's Life*. NY: W.W. Norton, 1991.

Corbin, Henry. *Avicenna and the Visionary Recital*. London: Routledge and Paul, 1961.

Crevecoeur, J. Hector St. John de. *Letters from an American Farmer and other essays*. Cambridge, MA: Belknap Press of Harvard UP, 2013.

Curti, Merle. "The Reputation of America Overseas (1776-1860)." *American Quarterly* 1.1 (Spring, 1949): pp. 58-82.

Gilbert, Alan. "Charles Olson and Empire, or Charles Olson flips the wartime script." Paper presented to the National Poetry Foundation Conference on American Poetry in the 1960s, University of Maine, Orono, July 2000. Text available on the Olson Now documents page, Electronic Poetry Center, http://epc.buffalo.edu/authors/olson/blog/Olson_and_Empire.pdf (last accessed July 2015).

Goldstein, Robert Justin. *Political Repression in Modern America from 1870 to 1976.* Cambridge, MA: Schenkman Publishing, 1978.

Hardt, Michael and Antonio Negri. *Empire.* Cambridge, MA: Harvard UP, 2000.

Howe, Susan. *The Birthmark.* Middleton, CT: Wesleyan, 1993.

Jennings, Francis. *The invasion of America: Indians, colonialism, and the cant of conquest.* Chapel Hill: U of North Carolina P, 1975.

Melville, Herman. *Moby-Dick, or The Whale.* Ed. Parker, Hershel, and Harrison Hayford. NY: WW Norton, 2002.

– *The Confidence Man: His Masquerade.* Ed. Parker, Herschel. NY: Norton, 1971.

Olson, Charles. *Call Me Ishmael.* [1947]. London: Jonathan Cape, 1967.

– "Captain John Smith." In *Collected Prose.* Ed. Donald Allen and Benjamin Friedlander. Berkeley: U of California P, 1997.

– *Charles Olson at Goddard College April 12-14, 1962.* Ed Kyle Schlesinger. Austin: Cuniform, 2011.

– *Charles Olson Reading at Berkeley.* Transcribed by Zoe Brown. San Francisco: Coyote, 1966.

– *The Maximus Poems.* Ed. George Butterick. Berkeley : U of California P, 1983.

– "Operation Red, White & Black." *OLSON, The journal of the Charles Olson archives* 5 (Spring 1976): 27.

– "The Vineland Map Review," In Collected Prose. Ed. Donald Allen and Benjamin Friedlander. Berkeley: U of California P, 1997.

Paz, Octavio. *The Labyrinth of Solitude: life and thought in Mexico.* NY: Grove Press, 1962.

Rowe, John Carlos. *The Cultural Politics of the New Amer-*

ican Studies. Ann Arbor: Open Humanities Press, 2012.

Scheidel, Walter. "Republics between hegemony and empire: How ancient city-states built empires and the USA doesn't (anymore)." Princeton/Stanford Working Papers in Classics. http://www.princeton.edu/~pswpc/pdfs/scheidel/020601.pdf. February 2006. Last accessed July 2015.

Sauer, Carl O. "Environment and Culture during the Last Deglaciation." Proceedings of the American Philosophical Society, Vol. 92, No. 1 (Mar. 8, 1948), pp. 65- 77.

Winthrop, John. "A Model of Christian Charity." In *Sermons that Shaped America*. Ed. Barker, William S. and Samuel T. Logan, Jr. Phillipsburg NJ: P&R Publishing, 2003.

– "On Liberty (The Little Speech)." The Constitution Society. http://www.constitution.org/bcp/winthlib.htm. Last accessed July 2015.

With gratitude to Daniel Zimmerman, Adrew Urie, Douglas Barbour, and Peter Quartermain for their invaluable and prodigious assistance.

Kenneth Warren

from: *Charles Olson
and the Examination of Empire*

Rhythm and the Recursive Wild Man

To account credibly for Charles Olson's life and work under empire, his rhythm must be experienced, his image assimilated, his language read, and his intentions remembered. In *Tramping the Bulrushes* (2006), John Clarke pursued "knowledge" (1) about the "rhythm" of Olson's opus and its propagation by means of an imperial optic keyed to "the antithetical influx of our time" (1). Demanded by disorienting affects released from Tom Clark's *Charles Olson: Allegory of a Poet's Life* (1991), Clarke's "self-correcting course" (1) of "scholarship" (1) sharply concentrated "knowledge" (1) about Olson's cultural representation and political position in an image and counteractive proposition poignantly expressed in Hakim Bey's *T.A.Z* (1991): "the Wild Man is lodged like a virus in the very machine of Occult Imperialism" (14). Out of control in the control matrix, as Clark suggests, Olson packed a "rhythmic (i.e. you had to be there)" (4) stress destined not only to go viral but equally to evoke hysteria, paranoia, and precarity amidst the Dark Lords of instrumental being who have been ruling the planet from Atlantis to America.

The connection Clarke made between Olson and "the Wild Man" holds up with stunning firmness when assaying *The Empire of Neomemory* (2013) by Heriberto Yépez and *A Little History* (2013) by Ammiel Alcalay. Side by side, these books look at Olson's propagation through an imperial optic that magnifies the overall history of colonial and postcolonial powers. The nervous wreckage that accumulates as poetry under empire is duly assembled in these books, which at the same time generate sufficient contrast for readers to differentiate between any cultural representation and any political position capriciously fused to Olson's rhythm. To make "knowledge" of any such fusion emphatic is, effectively, to resist confusion. Alcalay's *A Little History* makes clear that the "self-correcting course" of "scholarship" set in motion by Clarke must now confront "the Wild Man" within Heriberto Yépez, for his *The Empire of Neomemory* (2013) is wholly dependent upon [Tom] Clark's Charles Olson: *Allegory of a Poet's Life* (1991) to answer the question: "Can a biography explain an empire?" (11).

For a dot-connector like Yépez, who observes the United States from below in Mexico, the answer to this question is: of course. Olson is for Yépez a controlling image that gives meaning to his experience of North American cultural production. Through Olson he organizes his philosophy of empire and psychology of patriarchy. Quickly framing this question in reifying terms such as "an Oxidant that includes

Mexico" (12) and "The North American System" (16) that "compressed" (13) Olson's father in The Post Office (1948), Yépez advances through works imagined by Charles Bukowski and Ray Bradbury a novel conceit about "Going Postal" (11) in relation to "the foundation of the empire to come" (12). To make a long story short, a massive cybernetic metaphor of empire is juxtaposed to Olson's biography. The result is not persuasive but the performance is provocative.

Yépez is a psychotherapist. The epistemological and thematic premises that allow him to choreograph Olson's biography in connection with empire are broadly staked to general systems theory (Ludwig von Bertalanffy, *General Systems Theory: Foundations, Development, Applications,* 1968/1976). Joining the science of patterns, namely, cybernetics, to the practice of patterns, namely, systemic family therapy, he launches an outlandish intervention that factors out a great deal of what Olson actually said and wrote about empire.

"Rotten from the very beginning" (Diane di Prima, *Old Father, Old Artificer : Charles Olson Memorial Lecture,* 2012, 20) is how Olson characterized the colonial settlement of America in a conversation with Diane di Prima. The supreme law of the United States of America faired no better in his estimation, as di Prima reports: "Constitution written by a bunch of gangsters to exploit a continent" (20). Nevertheless, Olson's early gearing in the global idealism of Roosevelt can easily result in a conflation of his biography with internationalist dreams of empire and the globalist push to end the nation state. During World War II, the highpoint of cooperation between the United States and Mexico, Olson was involved in the ideological and strategic struggle to ensure pan-American unity. Through Roosevelt's "The Good Neighbor Policy" the pursuit of pan-American unity involved cultural and educational propaganda efforts that were coordinated by industrialist Nelson Rockefeller who led the Office of Inter-American Affairs. While performing under the jurisdiction of Office of Inter-American Affairs, Olson collaborated with photographer Ben Shahn to produce a bilingual pamphlet, *Spanish-Speaking Americans in the War* (Daniel Belgrad, *The Culture of Spontaneity: Improvisation and the Arts in Postwar America*, 1998, 24).

In the pamphlet there is a quotation from President Roosevelt concerning economic justice that states boldly: "We know that the day of exploitation of the resources and the people of one country for the benefits of any group in another country is definitely over." Elsewhere an internationalist effect is accomplished further through invocations of the United Nations and the human need for global food security. The progressive earth politics of Henry Wallace may also be heard in the pamphlet relating under a section titled "FOOD" that "in this global war we have learned the old lesson that the man who works the earth is basic to us all, soldiers, civilians and allies." Cited are President Roosevelt's remarks to the United Nations Food Conference. "The stores of the United Nations" are invoked in this capstone appeal to "Spanish speaking Americans":

The Spanish speaking American, heirs to the oldest agricultural tradition in America, are working with their hands and their machines to add the citrus fruits of California and Texas, the beet sugar of California and Colorado, the wheat of New Mexico and the cattle and sheep of the Rio Grande to the stores of the United Nations.

Olson's ideology of internationalist New Deal leftism was ultimately 'advertised out' of the Office of War Information. "The democratic possibilities of the New Deal had come to a close, and a corporate-advertising oligarchy was firmly in power" (25), writes Daniel Belgrad in *The Culture of Spontaneity: Improvisation and the Arts in Postwar America* (1998). However, Yépez claims that Olson was "fervid U.S. nationalist" (57). To charge Olson with nationalism in this way is to be thoroughly imprecise. With Yépez, though, "nationalist" is, like "empire," an empty slogan shorn of any content traceable to the historical sociology that informed Olson's choices, politics, situations, and statements. Again, when Olson declared the nation "rotten from the very beginning," he neither enshrined an ideal nor embossed the founding fathers in any spiritual principle—two crucial endowments for any nationalist exaltation.

In a stretch, when fathoming Olson's work within the Roosevelt administration, one might claim a modernist mode of civic nationalism, which occluded perhaps latent racialisms that bound Anglo-Saxon and Zionist interests to the Allied cause that fought against Germany and Axis nations in World War II. As a propagandist for the Office of War Information, he certainly served Allied war interests determined to break diplomatic and trade relations between Latin American nations and Axis powers while at the same time neutralizing within ethnic groups living in the United States any bonds that might incline them sympathetically toward enemy nations. On behalf of the democratic idealism and civic nationalism pivotal to a progressive Anglo-American ideology, his psychological warfare efforts were pitched at an emotional level to attenuate attachments that joined ethnic nationalities to tribes in Axis nations.

Olson had no sympathy for either the racial element or the imperial element through which the British elite sought to reclaim America, though. An indignant letter written to Ezra Pound in 1948 makes clear his opposition to "anglosaxonism," "academicism," and "empire":

BUT you have to deal with us Olsons... your damn ancestors let us in (AND AS ABOVE I DON'T THINK THE BATHTUB WAS SO CLEAN WHEN THEY DID). We're here. And to tell you your own truth, you damn well know anglosaxonism is academicism and shrieking empire. LIFE out of Yale, CULTURE out of Princeton, and the BOMB out of Harvard. (*Selected Letters*, 75-76)

In a letter written June 13, 1952, Olson attempted to pull Cid Corman back from international currents that were both advancing and mimicking United States imperial policy. Stressed is the connection between "the US EMPIRE'S" global resource extraction, cultural policy, and *Perspectives U.S.A.*, a magazine of art and culture edited by James Laughlin, underwritten by the Ford Foundation, and published in Europe:

Now one reason why yr fellow editors are fearful of Laughlin's HINDSIGHT, USA (the latest of the MARSHALL PLANS, and like those, "international," as the US EMPIRE is necessarily world-wide (Persian oil, Indonesian rubber, and the danger from the real masses—the Chinese, Indian, and East Russia) is precisely that Hutchins Etc (State Dept and Publishers) have swallowed up their premise. (*Charles Olson & Cid Corman: Complete Correspondence 1950-1964 Vol. 1*, edited George Evans, 1987, 268)

Elsewhere in this same letter Olson described the coordination of credit, monopoly wealth extraction, and technological control by power elites driving the war economy. Indeed, there is "Conspiracy," (270) claimed Olson, hardly an apologist for either the American empire or the Soviet empire. In Olson's dissident view, corporate state monopoly on the right and socialist state monopoly on the left were coupled in a system of war that was ultimately designed to limit productive capacity for the benefit of the many and by extension to maximize wealth accumulation for elites. To Corman, he writes:

The approximate identity of the Right and Left, that "Conspiracy": how to see how one system basing itself on credit and so limiting production in the face of its own technological forward motion comes more and more to resemble and collaborate (essentially) with another system, basing itself on an unobservable destitution of the masses, which consolidates all power in a political leadership and ends up expanding only those productions which enable it to oppose the other system in war—and so each comes, by the final act of itself, more to resemble the other than any common difference of the citizens of each. (270)

"Expression," figured Olson, could be deployed against the demobilizing simulacra of empire as "the only answer to the spectatorism which both capitalism and communism breed—breed it as surely as absentee ownership (whether of a leisure class or of a dictatorship, in the "proletarian" sense) doth breed it, separating men from action as surely as—as a leadership—these two identities limit production, or regulate it, in that monstrous phrase which turns all things toward creation's opposite, destruction"

(271). With the rise of mass media controlled by the corporate oligarchy, Olson could observe that, to use the phrase of Situationist Guy Debord, The Society of the Spectacle (1970/1977) was trashing the ideals of the democratic left. Astonishingly critical insights about how imperialism was playing out across the globe after World War II are also evident in Olson's *Selected Letters* (2000). Readers of Olson's letters will certainly recognize that "Olson leads us to the avatars of empire" (12), though not in the half-baked phanstasmorgia that Yépez constructs in *The Empire of Neomemory*. With far more political significance and understanding than Yépez can manage, "the avatars of empire" are laid out in Olson's critical analysis of monopoly powers generated in the back-and-forth flow of correspondence with others.

Letters, letters, letters...

Filled with gags *The Empire of Neomemory* is built by Yépez around his own love-hate relationship with connection and correspondence. His way of playing with Olson is to represent a defective character, because "he was a man who only seemed to think by means of correspondence (11). To flatten Olson into a defective character that replicates empire at "the cybermnemetic threshold" (5), Yépez must not only must strip down biographical and historical particulars but also deny the poet any deeper orders of correspondence with the cosmos. By reducing the bandwidth of "correspondence" to "the epistolary" (11), "the postal" (11), and "the army" (16), Yépez achieves the redundancy necessary to connect Olson's biography to an apriori metaphor of empire. His recursive churning factors so much out, though, that *The Empire of Neomemory* may be reasonably characterized as a dadaesque production of a "postal" (11) psychotherapist overcome by frame analysis.

There is no doubt that training as a psychotherapist lends support for inclinations to register symptoms, to reduce specifics to universals, and to weave life stories into metaphorical and recursive relationships. In the context of systemic family therapy, Yépez constructs an epistemology of complexity around biographical accounts of Olson's relationships with his father, mother, and lovers. With comic overreach to nullify, he cannot intervene effectively on Olson's behalf. Not bothering to read Olson's opus with any critical scruples, he admits that "Olson in and of himself does not interest me; I am interested in his character as a microanalogy for decoding the psychopoetics of Empire" (73). Wholly possessing Yépez is the apriori power to make meaning on the basis of an empire that erases memory and that cancels the author. Consequently, the determining imposition upon Olson's biography is "the North American system" (16), in other words, a totalizing unit of "compression" (16) determined by exchanges of "information" (17) between constituents of empire. Under this cybernetics model, Karl, Mary, and Charles Olson are mutually interrelated elements that exchange "information" (17) in a family structure "compressed" (16) by "the North American system" (16).

The distinguishing feature in the Olson family's identification with "the North American system" is "The Post Office." Olson's story about his father emits a signal from "the North American system" (16), a trans-positional signal at that, turning Yépez himself "postal" (18) in a recursive relationship with a not-so Merry Mailman cum G.I. Joe the Poet: "I want to highlight that Olson phrase, 'The postal system has resemblances to the army'—which takes new meanings once we understand his writing is 'postal' and thus resembles 'army'" (16). From this highlighted "phrase," Yépez proceeds to conscript Olson's contents, ethics, history, and politics into "the North American system" (16).

Beyond "the North American system" a far more global template is suggested by Olson's insight into the "resemblances" between the "postal system" and the "army." From the Persian imperial messengers noticed by Herodotus to the German model of bureaucratic capitalism advanced by Bismarck, the post office has been bound to empires, military operations, and utopian fantasies. During the Progressive Era in the United States, when the rejection of laissez-faire economics was underway, the particular term "postalization" emerged to signify a civic order of "nationalization," public service, and utopian experiment, in other words, an efficient and rational alternative to corporate capitalism, the history of which David Graeber identifies in *The Utopia of Rules: On Technology, Stupidity, and the Secret Joys of Bureaucracy* (2015). No matter how deeply connected an empire may be to a courier system, it is important to acknowledge that beyond the "resemblances" between the "postal system" and "the army" there persist profound differences concretely registered by the force of their interventions upon human lives.

To convey better the cybernetic implications of these "resemblances," which in *The Empire of Neomemory* frame Olson as a poet ultimately "guided by his mentality as a war veteran" (57), it should be stated further that for Yépez "the North American system" (16) is "the pattern which connects" (Gregory Bateson, *Steps to an Ecology of Mind*, 1972). "To understand his imperialist militarism," Yépez counsels, "one must de-translate him, since in Olson the imperialist militarism became a poetic, a metaphoric code, in short, *literature*: his war veteran's vision camouflaged itself until it became subtle poetry" (57). Because the imperial whole is greater than the sum of Olson's poetic parts, Yépez can make all the pieces fit into his own totalizing intervention fantasy. Tied all together in *The Empire of Neomemory* are "the North American system" (16), "imperialist militarism" (57), "linear history, Oedipal history" (33), "the fantasies of the pseudo-son," (33), "Pantopia," (33), "subtle poetry" (57), and, of course, Olson.

"The Unrelieved" Complexity of Memory

Alcalay's *A Little History* invites us to dig a little deeper into the formative pressures of American empire upon Olson. Significantly, Robert Duncan's important insight—"Olson's 1910 birth meant that he was born in a 'pre-World-War-world'" (92)—marks for Alcalay a turning point in the emergent imperial landscape. Pushed back to 1910 from the "1950s" (136)—the decade of "Neoeternity" and the "Military-Industrial Complex" (136) so heavily emphasized in *The Empire of Neomemory*—the date to begin examining Olson's biography and empire is the moment in history when the United States was becoming heir to the British Empire and when political Zionism was becoming increasingly enmeshed in an Anglo-American imperial vision of dominion and exceptionality. Indeed, in the United States of the 1910s the exceptionalist fantasy was the crazy glue that bound white Protestant fundamentalism and political Zionism to an ideological alliance thoroughly serviceable to the super-imperialism that would take hold of the Holy Land and the oil resources of the Middle East. Against the German industrial and military menace, moreover, American internationalists, British imperialists, banking dynasties, corporate plutocrats, and Zionists were all embedded in the capitalist push for a global financial empire resulting in a century of war. Almost at the jump, then, Alcalay succeeds in scoring the imperial sequence and "poetic knowledge" (12) necessary for a credible examination of Olson and empire.

Alcalay's extraordinary respect for the mission of "poetic knowledge" (12) to transmit moral registers against the historical reality of war marks a key difference between *A Little History* and *The Empire of Neomemory*. Arrayed to achieve instantly intelligible and reinforcing assertions about Olson and empire are Duncan's "generational mapping" and Muriel Rukeyser's observation of "the empire of business within the republic" (92) and "perpetual warfare" (92). The logistics of war thus coincide with the "poetic knowledge" that Alcalay cultivates. For Alcalay expurgated memory can never substitute for "poetic knowledge".

When Alcalay does consider the age of Pax Americana, which began in 1945, the very year that Olson had completed *Call Me Ishmael*, assumptions charged by ethics and history are brought sensibly to bear upon the crucial statement in "La Preface": "Put war away with time, come into space" (*Collected Poems*, 46). No territorial logic of imperialism is concealed in this statement. Signaled in "La Preface" is an outright rejection of war.

Arguing from a total war spatialization hypothesis in *The Empire of Neomemory*, Yépez frames Olson in "imperialism militarism" (57). In *A Little History* Alcalay brings historical pressure to get rid of the exaggeration. As Alcalay knows well, the elaboration of truth remains a possible function within Olson's endeavors. When the correspondence between Olson's thought about the justification for World War II and the objects of war broke down, a different matter of practice was demanded, as Alcalay argues:

The "big lie," Olson's interpretation of the result of war, was a bitter response to hopes he might have once held. I think he could not see himself partaking in what was coming, he saw very clearly what kind of machine was being put into place, a machine both beholden to and creating special interests, that was going to effect all aspects of life, especially the endeavor of research, of intellectual thought and activity, the transmission and location of knowledge. (111)

Extended in *A Little History* is the cultural complexity of the imperial landscape charted by Olson, with a particular focus on the foundational tropes of dominion, mercantilism, and ownership. "Olson was onto a lot of things," says Alcalay, pointing to "the elements out of which this country has mythologized itself and established itself and how that all actually works" (113). To be sure, Alcalay's treatment of Olson's "research and thinking about Melville, about Massachusetts, about the West and the gold rush, then Iraq and Mesopotamia, the Mayans, and the nature of the "West" as a whole" (113) secures a measure of trust against the shadow of suspicion that Yépez casts over "a market of hybrid artifacts "(117) that Olson's "inebriated angry bricolage" (117) made of different civilizations.

From Olson's "Billy the Kid," a review of *The Saga of Billy the Kid* (1925/1953/1999) by Walter Noble Burns, Alcalay leads us toward a deeper consideration of the historical realities of "accumulation," "misery," and "unrelieved action" (Collected Prose, 311)—all very necessary for assessing the aggrieved octave inside the heart that bellows "Gringo" in The Empire of Neomemory. He clarifies Olson's recognition that the American wound-scape remains an "unrelieved" dimension of identity, injustice, interests, memory, and trauma (Collected Prose, 311), saying that

Deeper questions of gender and patriarchy seldom get explored or expressed in their biographical, political, economic, historical, or mythological context and complexity. Meanwhile, things left by the wayside or that are swept under the proverbial carpet don't disappear. They just become, in Olson's words, "unrelieved." (152)

To great effect, the word "unrelieved" inside Olson's rumination on The Saga of Billy the Kid has provided Alcalay with one of those panoramic clues into Old World ethnic strife and New World free-for-all "values" (313) that were ultimately incorporated into the United States.

During the gilded age after the Civil War, when Billy the Kid drifted into the New Mexico territory, unbounded violence between warring Anglo factions accompanied the theft of property from Hispanic ranchers whose land grants had been issued by Mexico or Spain. Variously described as a race war waged by Anglos against Hispanics and as a religious war waged by Irish-Catholics against the English and Scotch-Irish, the Lincoln County War provides ample ground for exploring the contours of the "unrelieved" as well as for achieving a more sympathetic understanding of the racial memory that Olson has activated in Yépez.

In *The Saga of Billy the Kid* Burns offers a cultural representation that places him in a genealogy of blond and blue-eyed killers, thereby leading us into the ethnic and racial frictions that super-charge the "unrelieved action" (Collected *Prose,* 311) baked into Olson's sense of the United States:

Like all the noted killers of the West, Billy the Kid was the blond type...It was the gray and blue eyes that flashed death in the days when the six-shooter ruled the frontier. (60)

Invoking more than folklore and oral traditions, Burns then locates Billy the Kid within an evolving morphology of German and English heroes:

He is already in the process of evolving into the hero of a Southwestern Niebellungenlied. . . He is destined eventually to be transformed by popular legend into the Robin Hood of New Mexico—a heroic outlaw endowed with every noble quality fighting the battle of the common people against the tyranny of wealth and power. (69)

Having been dipped into a melting pot of Northern European heroes, Billy the Kid can stand as a figure capable of unifying ethnic strains between America's English and German populations in the period following World War I. Through a "transposition" (*Collected Prose,* 311) of German and English faces, however, *The Saga of Billy the Kid* leaves something "unrelieved" (*Collected Prose,* 311) about "the tyranny of wealth and power" (Burns, 69) in New Mexico. And so the story goes.

More recently, Billy the Kid has come to be considered an Irish-American outlaw hero, the son of Catherine McCarty, who arrived in New York City in 1846 in flight from the Irish Potato Famine. In "The Many Stories of Billy the Kid," Fintan O'Toole contends that the Lincoln County War was at bottom an extension of the Irish Catholic and British Protestant conflict into the New World (The New Yorker, December 28, 1998, 86-97). In view of O'Toole's account, the cattle rustling ways of the Scotch-Irish, who stole livestock from their English neighbors along the borderline of England and Scotland, before moving to Northern Island and then to America, underscore the tricky nature of ethnic and religious impulses that unfold from "man's interiors" (313) onto frontiers, extending toward in-group/out-group strategies of dispossession that inevitably lead to war.

During the days of Billy the Kid "unrelieved" Old World rivalries stirred inside Irish and English factions involved in the Lincoln County War. On the Irish side were Lawrence Murphy, James Dolan and the local sheriff, William Brady.

When wealthy Englishman John Tunstall enlisted former Murphy-Dolan employee Alexander McSween and cattle rancher John Chisum to compete with the highly profitable mercantile and banking monopoly known as "The House" the stage was set for war. Though Irish in heritage Billy the Kid worked as a gunman for Tunstall. When Tunstall was shot and killed by Dolan's ring on February 18, 1878, Billy the Kid was determined to avenge his death, allegedly remarking that "he was the only man that ever treated me like I was free-born and white" (Jay Robert Nash, *Bloodletters and Badmen: A Narrative Encyclopedia of American Criminals from Pilgrims to the Present*, 1995, 87).

Not surprisingly, Olson's use of the word "unrelieved" can direct our attention well beyond the "conversion" (*Collected Prose*, 313) of historical material into the myth of Billy the Kid. Against the background of the Wild West a deeper recognition of feelings about the racial and social hierarchies that stir madly within "man's interiors" (313) is now demanded. Carried forth from the Irish savage representation of Billy the Kid into the word "unrelieved" is an angle—at once ethnic, Freemasonic, and racial—pointing once again toward "the Wild Man ...lodged like a virus in the very machine of Occult Imperialism" (Hakim Bey, *T.A.Z.* 1991.Cited by Clarke, 14).

Since the 18th Century Freemasonry has accompanied the colonizing powers of British and French imperialism across the globe. To a high degree, Freemasonry established order on the chaotic frontier by means of charter, initiation, obligation, principle, ritual, secrecy, and symbol. In the homesteading

and incorporation of territory across the United
States, Freemasonry has long provided a set
of universal "values" that inspire members to pursue
career opportunities, commercial interests, and cross-
cultural civic ties, and esoteric knowledge. Within
the force of Anglo-American imperialism, moreover,
the connection between Freemasonry and military
strategy cannot be overlooked, as Robert W. Sullivan
IV illustrates in The Royal Arch of Enoch (2012):

In the United States, through the teaching of military
and civil engineering at West Point and Union College,
both deeply steeped in Masonic culture ... the
mechanistic idiom was extended through canalization,
railroading and telegraphy into the American frontier.
Similarly, the same inventions in Britain coupled with
the heritage of empire and navigation, the symbolic
naming process was extended through the powerful
capacities of imperial forces to establish persuasive
hegemonies over undeveloped regions. (xxxvii-xxxviii)

In the context of Billy the Kid and the closing of the
frontier, Freemasonry pinpoints an essential measure
for gauging the meaning of "unrelieved," particularly on
the basis of in-group and out-group membership. Simply
enough, the word "unrelieved" suggests the need for
relief, which is the duty of the Freemason.

Written in 1866 by Daniel Sickels, *The
General Ahiman Rezon and Freemason's Guide: Containing
Monitorial Instructions in the Degrees of Entering*

Apprentice, Fellow Craft and Master Mason (1871) instructs that

To relieve the distressed, is a duty incumbent on all men, but particularly on Masons, who are linked together by an indissoluble chain of sincere affection. To soothe the unhappy; to sympathize with their misfortunes; to compassionate their miseries, and to restore peace to their troubled minds, is the great aim we have in view (93).

To flash the secret distress signal of a Freemason is to call a brother to the duty of one's relief. The Freemasonic imaginary of charity, fraternity, and universality across the globe is clearly on offer here:

Masonry is a science confined to no particular country, but extends over the whole terrestrial globe... By secret and inviolable signs, carefully preserved among the fraternity, it becomes a universal language, Hence many advantages are gained: the distant Chinese, the wild Arab, and the American savage, will embrace a brother Briton, and know that, besides the common ties of humanity, there is still a stronger obligation to induce him to kind and friendly offices. (15)

In *The Saga of Billy the Kid* Burns does not examine the role that Freemasonry played in both the settlement and exploitation of territorial New Mexico. With the term "unrelieved," however, Olson offers a keyword for entering into the shadowy history of the Santa Fe Ring—"a loosely knit freemasonry of lawyers, soldiers, and Republican leaders with influential ties in Washington" (Frederick Nolan, *The Lincoln County War: A Documentary History*, 2009, 47). Most certainly, the Santa Fe Ring organized the legal and social injustice that Billy the Kid experienced in the murder of his employer John Tunstall. According to Nolan,

Most members of the Ring were Masons. Murphy and Dolan became the Lincoln County extension of this powerful group; indeed, Catron, Murphy, Dolan, and William Brady were among those who organized the first Grand Lodge in New Mexico. (47)

Needless to say, the murder of the wealthy Englishman in the New Mexico territory generated a significant volume of correspondence between United States and British elites. One rather interesting correspondent was Montague Leverson, a London born patent agent who had arrived in the United States in 1865. Prior to landing in the United States, evidently to provide "services to the Union," Leverson had been involved with European revolutionary secret societies (Frederick Nolan, *The Lincoln County War: A Documentary History*, 2009, 471). In fact, Leverson's home had once served as headquarters for Guiseppi Mazzini, Felice Orsini, and Giuseppe Garibaldi (471).

In a letter written on March 9, 1878 to President Rutherford B. Hayes about the Tunstall murder investigation and corruption in New Mexico, Leverson protested that "the Governor has illegally and despotically exerted his powers to screen the murderers." Indeed, Leverson's letter discloses that while membership in Freemasonry was a given among the power-brokers in the New Mexico territory the "spirit of the order" was violated in the process of the murder investigation because the foundational question of "truth" had been ignored:

Mr. Axtell is a freemason (so am I) and so is the Irishman who is here the leader of the thieves and assassins of this region, and I think it probable that in violation of the spirit of the order, the Governor has chosen to believe what his brother free-mason has told him instead of inquiring into the truth. (*The Life and Death of John Henry Tunstall* edited by Frederick Nolan, 2009, 295)

In New Mexico the principles of universal fraternity and enlightened civility professed by Freemasonry evidently provided ideological camouflage to corrupt self-dealing outlaws. So as not to leave any doubt about the composition of the "unrelieved" outside the Masonic lodge, though, membership in the secret society allowed the Irish as well as the English factions in the New Mexico territory to wage a "race war" against the Hispanic population, as Sue Schrems observes in "The

Billy the Kid Tintypes" (http://westernamericana2. blogspot.com/2010/01/billy-kid-tintypes.html). Thus the shadow side of the Freemasonic project gathers under the cover provided "thieves and assassins" determined to possess as much as possible from the incorporation of New Mexico territory.

To stand outside the lodge in the "unrelieved" situation of distressed Hispanic ranchers was to know intrinsically that the Masonic angle incorporated two lines — English and Irish — both coming from the single-pointed Anglo intention to gather property at their expense. By way of "the expansionary racism" that would eventually give rise to "globalization," moreover, Freemasonry afforded the Anglo factions in the Lincoln County War a strategic space that was far enough away from the dominant Hispanic population to allow them to plot successfully their respective shares in "the territorial gains" inspired by the Monroe Doctrine (David Harvey, *The New Imperialism*, 2003, 47). Obviously such a memory is necessary for appreciating the cultural representation of Olson that Yépez offers in *The Empire of Neomemory*. Likewise, Alcalay's attention to America's westward expansion and the Israeli frontier settlement in *A Little History* suggests that the "unrelieved" continues to fester underneath the legacy of British colonialism.

Compared with Yépez, Alcalay is capable of maintaining carefully considered historical attention to what remains "unrelieved" (152). Olson's recognition about invasion and dispossession in the United States resonates for Alcalay in the geo-politics of the Middle East. Having lived in Israel, he brings to "matters that have become more and more important, however forgotten, buried, or unrelieved they may be" (92) the intelligent grain of his own experience in "istorin," meaning "to find out for yourself" as in Olson's translation of Herodotus (*Mutbologos: Lectures and Interviews* 2010, 47). Immediately present in Alcalay's practice of "istorin" are "the enormous stakes in memory, where we place it, where it goes and what happens to principles over time" (92).

To get at the reality of "the unrelieved," Alcalay must concern himself with integrity and violation as matters for moral reflection and "poetic knowledge" (12). For Yépez, though, "poets are maximum errors" (128). "Poetic knowledge" (Alcalay, 12) is a laugh track. Left to poets "the unrelieved" becomes a laughing matter. Here the sadistic shrink goes one-up on "the amphibian of delirium" (127), sneering:

Consequently, poets deserve all our laughter—because everything they have done they have done in the name not of the gravity of truth, of the pseudo-life of negated death, but rather in the name of the disintegration of peals of laughter, the disintegration of truth, disintegration that begins with poets themselves, though they might not know it. The poets are here so we can laugh at them. (128)

What is barely contained in "the disintegration of peals of laughter" is the "unrelieved" superiority complex that plumes Yépez in his meditation on Quetzalcóatl, which he brazenly defines as "a *method* for achieving a superior state: metanoia" (138).

What the imperial sequence in *A Little History* ultimately assimilates is Alcalay's own personal experience with the "unrelieved" in Israel and Bosnia. Because the lines that define people and the lines that score poetry speak so deeply to Alcalay, *A Little History* takes on the dimensions of imperialism, militarism, and nationalism in ways that reveal particular contours of power not directly expressed in *The Empire of Neomemory*. While animus against the Gringo is strong in Yépez, his massing of homogenizing signifiers tends to scrub the deeper racial and religious charge from memory. Here, Alcalay's explicit attention to ethnic identities struggling for advantage, survival, territory, and self-determination over the course of history offers a strong contrast to *The Empire of Neomemory*.

As for the foundational Puritan/Hebraic culture that Olson inscribed in *The Maximus Poems*, it is connected in *A Little History* to the tragic dilemmas posed by "Israel's expanding occupation and influence" on what "became publicly imaginable, sayable, and real" (21). With Olson's claim that Melville understood "America completes her West only on the coast of Asia" in mind, Alcalay takes cognizance of the Vietnam War and Iraq War, writing:

Perhaps westward expansion for the United States reaches some apotheosis after the Vietnam War, with sneaker factories named after Nike, the Greek goddess of victory, and Babylon remade in our image, eradicating the likely site of Eden to displace it to the northwest, to the Middle East's "only democracy," that land of uprooted olive trees and legalized torture. (145)

In *from the warring factions* (2012), something of a precursor and companion book to A Little History, Alcalay considers through the war in Bosnia "the whole question of American empire, of obliteration and genocide of native people" (192). He goes on to say that "Americans are channeled into identifying with the Israeli pioneer, like the Wild West, and to distance themselves from Palestinians who, like Native Americans were removed from their land" (200). He speaks, too, of "the inordinate pressure from mainstream intellectuals in New York to evade the US relationship to the Middle East and alternative versions of Jewish history" (187).

In Alcalay's world, then, "Olson's tracks" engage a force of truth substantially grounded in commitments to community, correspondence, ethics, inquiry, justice, knowledge, and self-expression. Against "the cybermnemetic illusion" (6) presented by Yépez as Olson's "threshold" (6), Alcalay offers an identifying background that includes documents, events, poets, stances, and statements. Posited in Alcalay's identifying background are not only Olson's continuing international significance but also critical implications about "the poet's world" (16) under empire. With *The Empire of Neomemory* in view, Alcalay writes:

Despite recent critiques that would see Olson as the imperial outsider projecting the white world's fantasy upon non-white peoples, it is well nigh impossible to assimilate such readings into his lacerating critiques of North American imperial domination or his own actions in decidedly removing himself from access to power structures that were available to him. (201-2)

In *The Empire of Neomemory*, an exaggerated cultural representation of Olson as a "military imperialist" (57) results from the failure to distinguish ideological convictions, mythopoetic formulations, typological dispositions, and territorial dispossessions from one another. This cultural representation of Olson never quite escapes the unbounded domain of empty names, excessive abstraction, guilty projections, linguistic intricacy, inflated rhetoric, and theoretical excess that Raphael López-Perdraza has identified with Titanism in such books as *Cultural Anxiety* (1990) and *Dionysus in Exile: on the Repression of the Body and Emotion* (2000). Under Titanic pressure, there is no close textual analysis, little in the way of citations to be noticed in *The Empire of Neomemory*. It is no longer necessary to quote Spengler, Said, or Hardt and Negri. Empire and memory have been deconstructed, set adrift in language, sans rigor, sans everything.

"Everything will be postal." (12), announces Yépez ready to gun for Olson with a verbal arsenal packed with semiotic and technological jargon, from cultural studies, deconstruction, and postcolonial studies he hacks convictions about "the fragmentation of reality, experience, and memory," the accumulation of an "Oxcident that includes Mexico" (12), the information of "the world structured by syntagmatic dialogue" (13), "the telephysical structure of government (12), and "biocriticism of the geopolitical" (12). For this conceptual innovator, Olson's "WILL TO COHERE" (*Collected Prose* 1997, 172) is collapsible. With bravura, he pushes "blah-blah-blah" (López-Perdraza, *Cultural Anxiety*, 15) upon Olson's biography.

Broadly speaking, the Titanic template for "the cybermnemetic illusion" that Yépez brings to his reflection on Olson and empire stems from Jean Baudrillard's vision of America as a rootless civilization along with his idea of the "simulacrum"—reality without a referent. "Industrialized postmodernism" (85) is how Alcalay might describe the Orwellian world without memory pedaled by Yépez. For Alcalay, "a lot of the theoretical language and the way it's taught and how it's used is really colonizing, it's a subjugation of the material that it's supposed to be examining, and a kind of training in subjugation" (85). With an exacting interest in the referent, certainly the lynchpin in the old school historiography that Olson burnished into his opus, Alcalay offers crucial lessons for cutting through the Titanic "mimicry and excess" (López-Perdraza, *Cultural Anxiety*, 15) that possesses Yépez.

Not quite so ideologically bloated as *The Empire of Neomemory*, then, A Little History registers something as seemingly small as Alcalay's childhood memory of playing a backyard badminton game with the full-sized Olson. As a result, a vastly sympathetic overlay of mutual content is thereby interwoven into an examination of Olson and empire. Wrought by the power of this memory, *A Little History* presents a necessary step toward understanding the forgetting implied in the term "neomemory." In this memory, too, A Little History discloses something about Alcalay's own personal substance, which has been shaped by an interacting universe.

In playing badminton with Olson, Alcalay experienced a transmission of sorts, namely, the "rhythmic (i.e. you had to be there)" (4) influx that Clarke described in *Tramping the Bulrushes* (2006). By way of experience, Olson's "rhythmic" influx is now the memory calling through A Little History to "reanimate contexts" (17) in a spirit that "moves humanly close to the poet's world" (16). There can be no hiding from the psychic reality that has enveloped Alcalay and Olson in the neighborhood accretions of care, kinship, and presence that emotionally structure "the poet's world" (16). Here lies the communal basis for the gain in A Little History, with Alcalay and his editor Fred Dewey "transforming lectures projected at specific audiences at different times into a conceptual narrative" (259) that firmly insists upon biography, community, and history in a layered rendering of Olson and empire.

A Little History remembers an order of intuitive

knowledge attached to the realm of subtle unconscious perceptions and delivered by the brain's right hemisphere. Again the brain's right hemisphere is responsible for global attention and spatial relations, which were very much in play during Alcalay's badminton game with Olson. In *The Empire of Neomemory,* though, such neuropsychological vigilance is the culmination of Olson's "war veteran's vision" (57) (Iain McGilchrist, *The Master and his Emissary: the Divided Brain and the Making of the Western World,* 2009, 17, 171).

Of course, it is through the synthesizing powers of the right brain that memory feeds the aggregated totality of the Unus Mundus, the Noosphere, and other such constructs for holism. To recognize the difference between Olson and "the imperialist function" (Yépez, 59), it will suffice to remember that the Unus Mundus of "the Wild Man" is not derived from "the very machine of Occult Imperialism" (Bey quoted by Clarke, 14). Even though Olson's tone is brutal and foolish when communicating to Creeley about his encounters with Mayans in Mexico during the 1950s, he is revealing hidden aspects of "the Wild Man" in himself through the mechanism of projection.

Quite fundamentally, the equations that conflate Olson with empire in *The Empire of Neomemory* are based on a distrust of myth and a disregard for the synthesizing powers of the right hemisphere of the brain. Thus Yépez claims that

Myth allows Olson to allege that his models were Edenic, universal, primordial, ancestral, perennial. In his reconstruction of myths, Olson eliminates antithesis. He makes One of the many. In myth, Olson *fuses*. Synthesizes. (59)

For Yépez myth is Olson's military camouflage. While the cultural complex carried by Olson as an American took hold of his shadow in Mexico, his use of myth does not necessarily hold to the single meaning of "Americanization" (59). Nor is "Olsonian myth the senile project to realize forgetting for reformatting purposes" (234), as Yépez claims.

Olson's experience of myth may be better understood in terms of the microstructure of the brain. Like all myth, "Olsonian myth" (234) signals the involuntary primacy of the right hemisphere in the shaping his self experience, however offensive and ugly the revelation of unconscious contents may be. As McGilchrist explains:

The right hemisphere seems more engaged by emotional, autobiographical memories. It is hardly surprising that the 'sense of self' should be grounded with 'the Other', not as an entity in atomistic isolation: 'The sense of self emerges from the activity of the brain in interaction with other selves.' (88)

Under empire memory is subject to intensive pressure, as Yépez fairly claims. Amnesia, interpolation, psychic driving, propaganda, and simulation are all rife in the empire's battle for hearts and minds. Nevertheless, the processes of accumulation, analogy, empire, and memory are all wildly conflated in *The Empire of Neomemory*. In the grand pile-up of "neomemory" (284-86) there is little acknowledgment that memory, however fragile, is mapped to genetically-based brains. Furthermore, it is not far-fetched to claim from perspectives in archetypal psychology and neurology that memory is an emergent phenomenon possessed by psychic and neurological structures. Obviously an environment may be thick with analogical, imaginal, phenomenological, and political orders. Here, memory may function as an innately conservative medium that relates psyche and matter, something Yépez does seem to take into account. And sure enough, these neurological givens of accumulation and conservation may also assist through analogical thinking in the construction of imperial orders.

In contrast to Yépez, Alcalay places an unrelenting emphasis upon "the integrity of memory" (115). "Following WWII," he writes, "our most courageous North American poets, artists, and thinkers removed themselves from the restraining orders of Cold War vocabularies and structures, going underground to create their own channels of communication."(11). For Yépez, however, correspondence signifies the anti-social—"going postal" (12). "The foundation of the empire to come" (12), suggests Yépez, was accomplished through correspondence. When looked at from Olson's recognition of "the unrelieved," though, his attack on "the postalization" process of "co-fantasy"(12) is fatefully bound to the culture war between the Gringo and the Mexican.

For Alcalay, editor of The CUNY Poetics Document Initiative, correspondence is a mutual and ethical process within a range of creative endeavors that confront "the unrelieved." Alcalay sees more deposited in correspondence than a letter-writer's desire to relate to another. In discussing "how work moves between people and what kind of solidarity remains in the integrity of memory"(115), he points to a deeper fetching process by which succeeding generations may gather details and tap wisdom kernels necessary for the survival of human culture on the planet.

Deeper still in *A Little History* is Diane di Prima, who "has enacted a bulwark against the technology of materialist reductions of human intention and will, particularly in relation to works of art" (210). It is through di Prima's refusal "to relinquish possession over the mysteries"(210) that *A Little History* brings forth a correspondence agenda that stands wholly undiminished by "an infomeme of some cybermnemics" (14) that Yépez would promulgate as the crux of Olson's intention.

In *A Little History* the subject of "the mysteries" remains a specific value in a practice of poetry inextricably mingled with correspondence, revolution, and transfiguration. Here, di Prima's *Revolutionary Letters* (1978/1998) is the inspiration in *A Little History*. Equally indispensable to *A Little History* is "feeling" (207), which can never be ignored in the real commitments that poets make to one another in correspondence. It is by honoring di Prima's insistence on "mysteries" (210), "letters," and "feeling" (207) as formative to "poetic knowledge" (12) that *A Little History* gains for us a deeper understanding of the correspondence agenda that Yépez has sought to trash in *The Empire of Neomemory*.

Correspondence is the seal of the planets upon manifested things, as Paracelsus held. God to planet, like to like, person to person, letter to number, word to idea, and so forth—Olson's thinking about bonds of sympathy, correspondence, connection of all, and pre-existent form reflects the Neoplatonic synthesis of Plato and Aristotle. To a considerable extent, Olson's poetics retains the hermetic part of Renaissance thinking projected into the New World, as di Prima suggests in *"Old Father, Old Artificer": Charles Olson Memorial Lecture* (2012, 42-43). As the basis of magic, correspondence is a crucial power traceable to the mythology of Hermes, which moves the psyche in Olson's opus far more than Oedipus. However, no relation to the divine is permitted the North American poet's imagination in the master-slave dialectic governing *The Empire of Neomemory*. To make light of Olson's Neoplatonic trajectory in soul, Yépez offers smugly: "Life of a wounded Hermes; everything in him was remittance and postal hope" (12).

In reflecting upon Olson as "a wounded Hermes" (12), Yépez flattens his imagination into a postal conceit that insists on "language that no longer communicated with the divine" (55). Despite Olson's intent to render service to the divine through the hermetic art of poetry, Yépez must muscle his language into a global heap of "modern literature, the sciences, the arts, philosophy, and the mass media," which "constructs images that the sovereign (i.e. the State and capitalism) will assume as their own, attempting to form themselves according to what their slaves have imagined" (55).

As the deity of change, Hermes certainly figures into the first line of "The Kingfishers," a "deployment of myth" that Yépez deems "demagogic, exaggerated, and sententious" (59). Besides being called "he of the stone heap," Hermes is the deity presiding over Olson's "hunt among stones," which Yépez regards as "a searching among *stones,* that is, among the symbolic elements of the natural and the primitive"(41). For Yépez, Olson "hunted among archives" (57). Through "bibliographic investigation" (62), claims Yépez, Olson evaded "raw stones" (62). Even conceding such assertions about "The Kingfishers," Olson's search for creativity, phallic function, healing, and protection remains imaged well within the archetypal auspices of Hermes.

From the hermetic perspective that informed Olson's life and work, analogy is formed by chains of starry attraction entangled in the neurology that gives rise to poetic knowledge. In analogy, Yépez finds only "the workings of empire" (11). In a cosmological sense, correspondence does indeed speak to the structure of Olson's thought. Unable to grant to Olson an imagination propelled by the chain of correspondence within the hermetic tradition, Yépez pushes an entirely different point of view on his psycho-poetic performance, one that is clever, contemptuous, and false.

To achieve "poetic knowledge" (12) about Olson, "the mysteries," and the reality of empire, as Alcalay summons us to in *A Little History*, there must be capacity for empathic, social, and stellar understanding, which is "part of the right frontal lobe"(McGilchrist, 88). Cultivated through expanded interaction between self and other such capacity takes Alcalay far enough into the terrain of culture war and divine aspiration as to face the Levantine traditions of Zoroastrianism, Judaism, Christianity, and Islam. Having written *After Jews and Arabs: Remaking Levantine Culture* (1993), Alcalay perceives poetry "as part of a planetary consciousness"(12), as well as "part of the international decolonization movement, one whose significance 'post colonial' theories, the rhetoric of globalization, neo-liberal economics, and aesthetic 'appreciation' of 'global' poetry" often dispense with" (16). By reconsidering "the time when United States policy shifted completely towards Israel, following the June War of 1967, moreover, Alcalay presents another filter for examining the century of war.

Not only does the Middle East provide Alcalay with the cultural history, petroleum resources, sacred texts, and tribal politics demanded to make proper sense of Olson's project. A relational ground emerges, too, with all the crucial shaping from the structure of the brain into the language of poetry, its experience in community, and its claim on mysteries. Placed in a context of "poetic knowledge" and "planetary consciousness" (12)—a context that includes not only Mahmoud Darwish and Samih-al-Qasim but also Aimé Césaire, Diane di Prima, Robert Duncan, Timothy Clover, and Charles Olson—is "the specificity of language and Adonis's central role in redefining the Arabic language"(13). "In creating new communities of thought," Alcalay proposes, "another form of kinship could base itself on poetic knowledge" (13). In catching Adonis describe the 'total poem,' Alcalay allows us to recognize the totally human aspiration for connection, integrity, and wholes, which the right hemisphere of the brain ensures. Not to be confused with the "totalitarianisms" (99) that Yépez consigns to "Pantopia" (100), Adonis declares:

I call the 'total poem' a poem which ceases to be merely an emotional moment but becomes a global moment in which intuitions of philosophy, science, and religion embrace each other. The new poem is not only a new form of expression but also a form of existence. (13)

Whatever the differences between *A Little*

History and *The Empire of Neomemory*, whatever the culturalfilterstowhichthesebookssubjectOlson,asingle convergence point around the psychic functioning of intuition and feeling seems indispensible if one is to make any useful distinction between: 1) individual abilities to formulate intention in a world under empire and; 2) ideological convictions about empire that function to deny personal intention, perception, and meaning. As Jungian analyst John Giannini has described in *Compass of the Soul: Archetypal Guides to a Fuller Life* (2004), the coupling of feeling and intuition supports the psychological experience of life as "a seamless whole since the feeling function seeks harmony among all and intuition embraces wholeness" (197).

The character of memory revealed in *A Little History* is reflected in the image of Olson at play as well as in the archetypal dimension of the divine child. From Gloucester to the Middle East the image of the divine child is "the carrier of imagination" (James Hillman, *Emotion: A Comprehensive Phenomenology of Theories and Their Meaning for Therapy,* 1960, xv). Stimulating the functions of feeling and intuition to flow together with caring attention to life, the divine child imaged in Samih al-Qasim's "Kafr Qasem," a lamentation for Palestinians villagers massacred in Galilee, and in Timothy Clover's "The Gift," a poem set in wartime Vietnam, inspires Alcalay to fathom more deeply the sorrowful heart of poetic reality under empire. From Olson to Adonis, from Duncan to Samih al-Qasim, from di Prima to Clover, Alcalay displays an appreciation for the poet under empire. By doing so he responds soundly to the unqualified notion in *The Empire of Neomemory* that "the poet is the amphibian of delirium" (127).

ED. NOTE:

Kenneth Warren was unable to provide a conventional bibiography for his essay. Most of his citations, however, address primary sources already mentioned in the text.

CORRESPONDENTS

John Stilgoe is a historian and photographer who is the Robert and Lois Orchard Professor in the History of Landscape at the Visual and Environmental Studies Department of Harvard University, where he has been teaching since 1977

Etel Adnan: "I don't think Olson would like today's Paris, or if he ever did. I wish he were around and would tell me something about the incredible violence that's eating the whole world nowadays. Probably nothing."

Ricardo Cázares, author of three collections of poetry including the long poem simply titled ◇, writes from his desk in Huixquilucan, Mexico, where he is currently proofreading his translation of the second volume of *The Maximus Poems*, the first complete Spanish rendering of Charles Olson's epic.

Murat Nemet-Nejat writes, still from this side of the grave, sporting a last name suggesting an aura of nonexistent nobility.

Claudia Moreno Parsons writes from Brooklyn, with love.

Susan Thackrey is the author of the book of poetry, *Empty Gate*, as well as *George Oppen: A Radical Practice.*

Alana Siegel dizzies a cosmos of kinship.

Tom Cheetham writes from a state of perpetual astonishment, where all times and places are contiguous, infinities touch, and everyone follows the footsteps of an Angel, out ahead.

Cole Heinowitz is writing from Kingston, New York, where she lives. She gave this letter to a friend, who delivered it to Gloucester.

Jeff Gardiner writes from a room looking out over the hills and coast inhabited by the Ohlone (or Costanoan) Native American people before Spanish explorers and missionaries began the developments that would lead eventually to the new empire of mis-centered digital devices and a planetarium under a living roof.

Charles Alexander writes with a cat on his lap from a room in a home he shares with an artist in a Texas city (Victoria) new to them, after a life shared in a desert city (Tucson), long after a birth surrounded by ocean.

Basil King writes: "I wrote the letter Dear Charles two weeks before my eightieth birthday and sixty-four years after being his student."

Ruth Lepson writes from the snowbound city of Cambridge, MA, from where she goes up Rte 128 to Gloucester, ruining, with many others, the polis Olson loved.

John Smith, founder and former keeper of the Virginia Colony, writes from the library he shares with an ancestor of **Tyrone Williams**, a free black he mocks for "peering" at his collection of navigation and field guides....

Dale Smith lives and writes in Toronto, ON. *Slow Poetry in America* (Cuneiform 2014) is his most recent book. He is co-editor of a new quarterly newsletter, also called *Slow Poetry in America.*

Joe Safdie writes from a small office with a window that looks out over a cherimoya tree, a lantana plant, and a lemon tree (from left to right) in Encinitas, California. He mostly writes on a MacBook Air.

"**Hannah Arendt** writes from the household of **Joshua Corey**, author of *The Barons* and *Hannah and the Master*, a forthcoming fantasia on the romance between twenty-first century replicants of Hannah Arendt and Martin Heidegger."

Yorio Hirano is a professor of Sugiyama Women's' University, Nagoya, Japan. He translated The Maximus Poems into Japanese in 2012.

Ed Sanders is writing from a house on a mountainside in Woodstock, New York, striving to complete a long long poem on the final years of Robert Kennedy.

Peter Anastas writes from his desk in a room overlooking the Atlantic Ocean in Bass Rocks, Gloucester, MA, where the roar of the breakers often drowns out his thoughts.

David Rich is writing from a northern neighborhood of Gloucester, Massachusetts, where packs of coywolves roam the grounds of abandoned quarries.

Ammiel Alcalay's words are from his introduction to Amiri Baraka's talk, "Charles Olson and Sun Ra." Fourth Annual Charles Olson Memorial Lecture. Cape Ann Museum, Gloucester, MA. 19 October 2013.

Amiri Baraka's words are from: "Charles Olson and Sun Ra." Fourth Annual Charles Olson Memorial Lecture. Cape Ann Museum, Gloucester, MA. 19 October 2013.

Jack Hirschman is writing from his writing room in the Columbus Hotel in North Beach, San Francisco

Carla, the letter b. writes from a name that is not her own.

Michael Boughn writes: "Charles Olson was there, at the the beginning of the world. The conversation that started then will still be going on when it ends."

The late poet, scholar, and editor, **Kenneth Warren**, author of *Captain Poetry's Sucker Punch: a Guide to the Homeric Punkhole: 1980-2012*, wrote from a cottage on the happy shores of Lake Ontario in Ransomville, New York.

www.ingramcontent.com/pod-product-compliance
Lightning Source LLC
LaVergne TN
LVHW051726080426
835511LV00018B/2913